NONVIOLENCE AND CHRISTIAN FAITH

Published under licence by Brown Dog Books and
The Self-Publishing Partnership Ltd, 10b Greenway Farm, Bath Rd,
Wick, nr. Bath BS30 5RL

www.selfpublishingpartnership.co.uk

ISBN printed book: 978-1-83952-569-8
ISBN e-book: 978-1-83952-570-4

Cover design by Kevin Rylands
Internal design by Andrew Easton

Printed and bound in the UK

This book is printed on FSC® certified paper

This book is a substantially revised and significantly expanded version of my previous
book with a similar title, *Nonviolence and Christian Faith – a Challenge*, published by
New Generation Publishing in 2019

NONVIOLENCE AND CHRISTIAN FAITH

The Way of the Cross

MICHAEL ROGERS

For Judith, with love

and in memory of my parents
Geoffrey and Dora Rogers

Acknowledgements

My wife Judith, bless her, has been a constant source of encouragement while I have been writing this book.

I would like to thank my sister and brother-in-law Catharine and Andrew Wigram for their interest and support; and my cousin Rosalind Muston, for her enthusiasm in 'spreading the word' about my writing.

Bishop John Perry and his wife Marylin have not only been extremely supportive, but also agreed to write the Foreword. I am most grateful to them both.

Stewart Rapley offered an insightful critique of how best to get my message across. This led to some important re-writing of parts of the manuscript, to the benefit of the whole.

From his own extensive publishing experience, my son Seb has offered both encouragement and invaluable insights into the strange world of publishing in a digital age.

Last, but most certainly not least, I want to thank the team at Self-Publishing Partnership. Their expertise, needless to say, has been essential. They have all been a pleasure to work with, and they seem to me to have done the 'hard graft' bits of bringing this book to life and to market. It would not have happened without them, nor would the whole experience have been such a positive one.

Foreword

By Bishop John Perry, former Bishop of Chelmsford.

It is rare today to find a book that tackles the whole issue of nonviolence and Christian faith. It has only been in retirement from a busy life as a medical doctor that Michael Rogers has had the opportunity to bring this book to birth. His Christian faith, with passionate and personal conviction that violence is never in line with Christian faith, started from an early age. The author's book could not be more timely at a point when violence globally and nationally often dominates the headlines.

With sensitive and scrupulous research, he highlights the Early Church's rapid growth and largely nonviolent stand following the example, life and teaching of Jesus.

He also traces the Church's chequered periods over the centuries, including appalling abuse of power and coercion, including violence. Helpfully the author addresses many controversial perspectives and questions which he unpacks with courageous conviction.

"Nonviolence is the use of peaceful means, not force, to bring about political or social change" – these words were Gandhi's commitment to the principal of nonviolence.

This book underlines that organised and disciplined nonviolence can disarm and change the world, our lives, relationships and our communities.

Jesus reminds us, in the Sermon on the Mount, that "blessed are the peacemakers, for they shall be called the children of God".

A challenge to every reader.

Contents

References which include text notes are indicated with an asterisk, e.g. (2*)

Bible quotations are from the New Revised Standard Version

Introduction

I'd like to explain briefly what this book is about, and how it came to be written.

I'm a lifelong disciple of Jesus, now retired from gainful employment (I've discovered, by the way, that walking the dog every day, come rain or shine, is also a wonderful opportunity to walk and talk with Jesus). Seventy years ago, as a result of experiences at school (described in Chapter 1), I made a commitment to nonviolence as a guiding principle in my life. I obviously had Christian nonviolence firmly in mind, but at the time and subsequently I didn't work out in any detail what that really meant, other than looking into Quaker history, attending Quaker meetings for worship for several years, speaking my mind when opportunity presented itself, and trying constantly to think and act nonviolently. National Service was discontinued before I had the opportunity to register as a conscientious objector, which would otherwise have been a milestone. Pursuing a medical career and becoming jointly responsible for a new family seems to have taken up most of my time for most of my adult life, but those are poor excuses for not having been much more proactive, much earlier, about nonviolence.

In the more recent past, however, easing into retirement with an enquiring mind still intact, and blessed with good health, I found myself at last with time to take stock. I've used some of it to become a more involved family member, some to build and sail a couple of boats, quite a lot to make and listen to music, and more still to contribute to the life of our local church. Above all, I've taken time to be quiet, to think and read and pray, and to address important questions about my faith, an exercise which was long overdue. These questions included what is this nonviolence thing actually about? What does the Bible, and especially Jesus, have to say about it? How does it relate to my faith? What should its impact on my discipleship be? If it's important, why does 'mainstream' Christianity pay it so little attention?

It's been a fascinating, and in some ways disturbing, journey. It quite quickly became clear that, although what I discovered was new to me, as I think it will be to most Christians - which in itself is remarkable -- I was actually mining a deep and rich seam of spirituality going right back to the teaching and example of Jesus, to the discipleship of the Early Church, and to the faithful witness through the centuries of those relatively few Christians who have believed in nonviolence and have often suffered dreadfully as a result - as Jesus did.

These studies have made such a difference to my own faith that I found myself wanting to share my discoveries with as many people as possible. There's a degree of urgency about this feeling which surprised me, because I'm not usually a very outgoing person. I eventually realised that this desire to communicate came from the Holy Spirit who has, I now firmly believe, commissioned me to write this book. So that's how I came to write it, and you, of course, to read it.

Jesus had a lot to say about active nonviolence, especially in the context of conduct befitting his coming Kingdom (2). So, for example, 'love your enemies (Mat 5.44; Luke 6.27,35); bless those that curse you (Mat 5.44; Luke 6.28); do good to those who hate you (Mat 5.44); be merciful, just as your Father is merciful (Luke 6.36); do to others as you would have them do to you' (Luke 6.31). Jesus was himself the supreme example of nonviolent behaviour, both in his conduct during his human life, and as he went to his death (Isa 53.7, 1 Pet 2.21–23). In this, as in everything else, he 'walked the walk'. He also made clear what he requires of his disciples. We're to love God wholeheartedly, and to love our neighbour as we would love ourselves (Luke 10.27). In following him, wherever that takes us, we each have our cross to carry (Luke 9.23) – of which more anon. In the parable of the Good Samaritan Jesus deliberately conflated 'neighbour' and 'enemy' (Luke 10. 30–37) (3*), and we're required to '"go and do likewise' (Luke 10.37). In the Great Commission (Mat 28.19–20), note in particular the instruction that we're to teach all nations 'to obey everything that I have commanded you'. Related themes of love, humility, compassion, forgiveness and reconciliation run like interwoven golden threads through the Gospels, and are further developed in the Epistles, particularly those of Paul and John.

Perhaps the ultimate nonviolent metaphor in the Bible is in its final book where, in one of John's visions, the Lion of

Judah is transformed into the Lamb of God (Rev 5. 5–6). Of all things, a sacrificial *lamb* – what could possibly be more nonviolent than that?

This was the Gospel and model of discipleship which the early Christians took into the pagan, militaristic and at times virulently hostile world of the Roman Empire. They had astonishing success for three and a half centuries. Then, as we shall see, things changed, and very much for the worse. So, what went wrong? Why does the Church's history after the 4th century include lots of violence, some of it extreme, lasting 13 further centuries? In more recent times, why has the Church been almost universally complicit in national military conflicts? Since the emergence of modern nation states, why have Christians felt able to involve themselves in state violence, including service in the armed forces; and, by acquiescence at least, in the development and stockpiling of weapons of mass destruction? Where was the loud and unequivocal voice of Christian protest when the UK government recently (March 2021) suggested a 40 per cent increase in the number of nuclear warheads to be deployed by the UK's armed forces? I for one didn't hear it. Did you? Given the Church's past and present complicity in violence, an association which it scarcely acknowledges, how can it even begin to be an effective resource for national and international reconciliation? Why are most Christians apparently unconcerned about these issues? And what should those of us who are concerned actually *do* about it?

That's a lot of questions, none of them trivial. To try to tackle at least some of them, I've looked at the commitment of the Early Church to nonviolence, and why, when and how it morphed into violence. I've put together an overview of the Church's subsequent violent history. I've examined the firm grip violence has on the human condition, which is every bit as strong today as it has ever been. I'm perturbed by the silence (or is it just indifference?) of the Church about these issues. And if nonviolence is ever again to become a key part of the Gospel and of discipleship, as it certainly was for the Early Church (see Chapter 2), there is work to be done, and I've tried to suggest what that might mean.

I must re-emphasise that what I've discovered is not new, but it seems to have been largely ignored, to an extent depending partly on where people live. Anabaptist Mennonites, among others, already promote and practise nonviolence (1*). The relatively large groups in the USA and Canada contribute both thriving Church fellowships and academic teaching and writing within colleges and seminaries, producing books and other material on Christian doctrine, ethics, discipleship and Church history, all with a built-in nonviolent perspective. They are indeed the exception to the rule of general indifference about these issues, and their local and national witness must be invaluable. Sadly, there is nothing equivalent in size or influence on this European side of the 'pond', where there is a relatively small UK Anabaptist Mennonite Network (with links into several theological colleges), the steadfast peace testimony of the Society of Friends (Quakers) and a very few very small denominations with a historic commitment to peace. I do hope that there is also at least a sprinkling of individuals such as myself, both in the UK and in churches throughout Europe and beyond, who are personally convinced about the spiritual and practical importance of nonviolence.

To avoid possible misunderstandings, it may help if I make clear how I use certain terms in what follows.

- **Nonviolence** is, at its most basic, an absence of violence; but it can and should also be something much more positive, a dynamic concept with pervasive consequences.

- **Church** unavoidably has several meanings. In general, it means all people here on Earth who acknowledge Jesus as Saviour, and as the Son of God in a Trinitarian sense, with no particular denomination implied. Such a Church is diverse (which doesn't matter at all), and also disunited (which matters a lot). The Church is the body of all believers on Earth. It's also an institution, or a series of institutions. All these various 'templates' should fit snugly together. Sadly they don't.

- **Early Church** specifically describes the church up to about AD 350.

- **Christendom** refers to the amalgamation of Church and State after about 325, and to the various configurations of church/state union, initially Catholic but later also Protestant, which developed as a consequence during the following centuries.

- **The Way of the Cross,** in both title and text, is shorthand for the ongoing experience of any disciple of Jesus who picks up his/her cross daily to follow him (Luke 9.23: see pp 108–109). I couldn't find a better or more succinct way of referring to discipleship-with-potential-for-suffering, which is clearly what Jesus meant. (The more traditional use of the phrase, of course, is in the context of the Jesus-centred meditations on the Way, or Stations, of the Cross on Good Friday.)

- **Powers** and the **Domination System** are terms which are explained on pp 64–66. In the context of violence, these networks of 'influences and institutions', as Walter Wink (28) described them, are sufficiently important to be accorded capital initial letters throughout this book.

'We Will Kill
the Enemy'

Not long after the end of WW2, at the age of 13, I went to a boys' boarding school where the pervading ethos was that of personal Christian faith. There was emphasis on self-discipline, service to others, and kindness. Bullying was as much a 'crime' as cheating. It was taken for granted that a boy might wish to kneel by his bed in the dormitory to pray. Most of the teaching staff were committed Christians. The whole school attended chapel twice every day. Sunday sermons were overtly evangelistic, and senior boys led a lively Christian Union. A huge Honours Board in the main hall listed all old boys who had served abroad as Christian missionaries, a roll call going back over 80 years. The school was in many ways a remarkable place.

Other regular school activities included a combined cadet force (CCF), always referred to as 'Corps'. This was compulsory (except for a handful boys who did not participate, either because they were physically unable to do so, or were from Quaker or similar backgrounds). Corps was officered by members of staff who had been in the armed services during WW2, and by retired army personnel living locally: senior boys were NCOs. Every boy was assigned a full battledress uniform with cap and army boots, and took personal responsibility for an ex-WW1 rifle. The armoury hut, a long, low corrugated iron building, housed about 300 40-year-old rifles, and a few bren and sten guns. Most, but not all, these weapons were without their firing pins. Coincidentally, the door at one end of this arsenal was 25 yards from the corner of the school chapel. For about five hours every week, plus a whole field day each term (and a voluntary one-week camp during the summer school holidays, which I never attended), we paraded, drilled and obeyed orders; *and we were taught to kill.*

I'm not exaggerating. We learned and practised the basics of infantry tactics in the field, using stock scenarios such as 'the enemy is behind that hedge: we will kill the enemy, by right (or left) flanking'. We were taught what to do to the enemy – kill him, unless of course he surrendered first – and what the enemy would otherwise do to us. We talked about bayonet drill. Occasionally we fired live .303 ammunition on the school rifle range. The intention was to make Corps activities as militarily realistic as possible, given its part-time basis in a school setting.

It was assumed, without any discussion, that behaving in this way could, somehow, be squared with 'love your enemies' (Luke 6.35), 'turn the other cheek' (Mat 6.39) and the supreme example, 'Father, forgive them' (Luke 23.34); that it could be reconciled, in fact, with the active practice of Christian faith which pervaded the rest of school life. Even to attempt this, it seemed to me, meant that we had to switch off being Christian – by which I mean following the teaching and example of Jesus – while we learned to exercise morally mindless obedience on the parade ground and behind a gun; and then to switch on again when we resumed the rest of school life. It never seemed to occur to anyone, least of all to the school chaplain, with whom I tried unsuccessfully to discuss my concerns, and who acted as an enthusiastic umpire during Corps field days, that all this flew in the face of everything else which that particular school outstandingly stood for. I simply couldn't make sense of the incongruity; nor indeed of the strange fact that I seemed to be the only person in the school who was sufficiently bothered to make an issue of it. (Years later I discovered that several teachers had been supportive of my point of view.) A few boys were enthusiastic about Corps, becoming NCOs; the rest went along with it as just another activity which happened as a weekly ingredient of school life.

In my third term at school, during a Corps session out in the sunny countryside, I was instructed, amongst other things, to aim my rifle fire at 'the enemy's belly, not his heart. It's a bigger target', we were told; 'and even if you don't kill him on the spot, he won't be any good for fighting after that'. I remember that particular moment vividly as a tipping point. (I also remember that one of my group had the basic decency to mutter 'yuck!' under his breath.) It was suddenly obvious to me that as a disciple of Jesus I could never do anything remotely like that to another human being, under any circumstances whatsoever. I therefore decided that I had to make a stand, and I eventually succeeded in getting myself withdrawn from involvement in the CCF. Incidentally, for an otherwise unassertive first year pupil to insist on opting out of a major compulsory school activity, and one which no one else found objectionable, was much more difficult than it may sound.

*   *   *   *   *

The First World War, the 'war to end all wars', ended in 1918. Twenty years later global warfare erupted again as WW2. Both conflicts threatened the entire world order, and caused unparalleled destruction and suffering. Before and since then, *wars of all kinds and magnitudes continue to be waged somewhere on this planet*, every single one of them another self-inflicted wound injuring humankind (see pp 36–37). The events I've described here took place 70 years ago, which was a mere eight years after the end of WW2. One might have expected that even a smidgen of 'learning from history' would have discouraged the setting up of CCFs in schools to promote warlike attitudes, and presumably to try to make the armed services attractive to impressionable adolescents. Least of all, perhaps, might one have expected such activities in an otherwise truly Christian school. Well, 70 years on, my school (now co-educational) still has a CCF, which includes girl pupils and has naval and air force sections as added attractions. In the UK as a whole, the number of cadet forces in state (that is, not private) schools has more than doubled in the past ten years: the UK government funds the promotion of a military ethos in schools: and the UK is the only Western country to recruit 16-year-olds into its armed services (see pp 43–44). Lessons are obviously not being learned, but sadly there is nothing new about that.

The Nonviolent Church

To find out what happened historically to Jesus' teaching about nonviolence, we must first go back to its New Testament beginnings, to the Sermon on the Mount and the story of the Good Samaritan, to Jesus' Crucifixion and Resurrection, and to Pentecost. From there we need to look forward, through the period when the Bible record comes to an end, and to the times when the apostles and others who had known Jesus personally were no longer alive to give a lead. The Church thereafter had two particularly striking features.

The first was its rate of growth which was, quite simply, phenomenal. As we shall see later, by the 4th century Christians were numerically a significant minority, possibly even a majority, of the Roman Empire's total population. Rodney Stark examines how this happened in some detail in his book *The Rise of Christianity* (4*). Because his approach is academic rather than faith based, it is understandable that his intriguing, detailed and plausible analysis of this expansion doesn't include what to a Christian is the most obvious and important contributary factor of all – that this was the work of the Holy Spirit.

The second important characteristic of the Early Church was that *it was nonviolent*. It doesn't seem to be widely known that this burgeoning movement within the militant and martial Roman Empire developed *a strict and universal discipline of nonviolence*, and maintained it for at least three and a half centuries (5). In historical terms, that's a similar time span to that between the Civil Wars in 17th century England and today; and it's only 50 years shorter than the entire history of the United States from the landing of the Pilgrim Fathers. It's noteworthy that, although the different centres of Christian belief within the Empire took time to achieve a degree of uniformity in their organisation, practices and doctrine, they appear to have spoken with one voice throughout this period on the issue of nonviolence. To all of them it was clearly a direct continuation of the teaching and example of Jesus, passed down in the oral tradition of the early post-Resurrection period, confirmed in the Gospels, and promulgated and practised by all Christians thereafter. This consistent pacifism was indeed one of the Early Church's most distinctive qualities, and must have been in stark contrast to the relentless militarism of the so-called *Pax Romana*.

Influential Early Church Fathers were consistent in their assertions that nonviolence was a *sine qua non* of Christian discipleship, as these quotations from their writings (5) make clear:

> **Justin Martyr** (about 150 AD) – We who once murdered each other indeed no longer wage war against our

enemies: moreover, so as not to bear false witness before our interrogators, we cheerfully die confessing Christ.

Tertullian (198–201) – First, can any believer enlist in the military? Second, can any soldier, even those of the rank and file or lesser grades who neither engage in pagan sacrifices nor capital punishment, be admitted into the church? No on both counts – for there is no agreement between the divine sacrament and the human sacrament, the standard of Christ and the standard of the devil, the camp of light and the camp of Darkness. One soul cannot serve two masters – God and Caesar … how will a Christian engage in war – indeed, how will a Christian even engage in military service during peacetime – without the sword, which the Lord has taken away? For although soldiers approached John to receive instructions, and a centurion believed, this does not change the fact that afterward, the Lord, by disarming Peter, disarmed every soldier. (6*)

Hippolytus (199–217) – A soldier, being inferior in rank to God, must not kill anyone. If ordered to do so, he must not carry out the order, nor may he take an oath (*sacramentum*) to do so. If he does not accept this, let him be dismissed from the church … Anyone bearing the power of the sword, or any city magistrate, who wears purple, let him cease from wearing it at once or be dismissed from the church. [Purple garments designated an *imperator* (commander and emperor), and wearing the royal colour, declared Hippolytus, blasphemed

Christ] … Any catechumen or believer who wishes to become a soldier must be dismissed from the Church because they have despised God.

Origen (248) – We must delightfully come to the counsels of Jesus by cutting down our hostile and impudent swords into ploughshares and transforming into pruning hooks the spears formerly employed in war. So we no longer take up the sword against nations, nor do we learn war anymore, since we have become children of peace, for the sake of Jesus, who is our leader, instead of those whom our ancestors followed.

Becoming identified as a Christian in these early years involved applying to join the Church, having the application accepted, receiving instruction in the basics of the Christian faith (catechism) and, finally, being baptised as a consenting, believing adult. The stringent conditions attached to accepting applications from people in certain occupations make it clear that the nonviolence of the Church at this time was far from a mere posture. Anyone seeking baptism, whose employment directly or indirectly involved violence or the taking of life, had to resign and find alternative employment before the Church would admit them. This most obviously applied to soldiers, but was extended to those in civilian posts, such as magistrates, who might be involved in administering the death penalty. (See the comments of Tertullian and Hippolytus above.)

The oath – *sacramentum* – which all Roman soldiers were required to take when they enlisted presented the church leaders with a particular challenge, because it was more than a promise of loyalty to the Emperor. It also bound the oath taker to the gods which, since the reign of Augustus, had included the Emperor as one of the deities in the Roman pantheon. It was, in fact, overt idolatry. (Only Jews were exempted from Emperor worship, with the proviso that they were required to pray *to* their one God *for* the well-being of the Emperor.) The clash between Christian baptism and the *sacramentum* was obvious, and was further highlighted whenever the highly seditious early Christian claim that Jesus was King – and therefore, by implication, that Caesar wasn't – surfaced, as it did from time to time.

This coherent and consistent emphasis on nonviolence was maintained by the Early Church until well into the 4th century. At some point it must have started to change; exactly why, how, and how quickly or, indeed, slowly, is not entirely clear. However, its synchrony with the Emperor Constantine's growing interest and intervention in Church affairs was certainly not coincidental (7)(8).

Considering his historical importance, Constantine comes down to us as a strangely enigmatic figure (8), with much of his life shrouded in a fog of mystery and controversy. On the one hand, there are churches where he is still revered as a saint, and as an example of a Christian monarch. On the other hand, he stands accused by some historians of having had his wife, eldest son and father-in-law murdered (it has to be said that such events were not that rare in Roman families with ambitious members in the upper echelons of political life and society). His formal conversion to Christianity is usually dated

312, although, unusually, he did not become a catechumen (someone receiving instruction with a view to baptism) until more than 25 years later, shortly before his baptism and death in 337. His Edict of Milan in 313 decriminalised all religions, obviously including Christianity, in the Empire. This brought to an official end the persecution of Christians for their faith, and bestowed a freedom which must have been celebrated with great relief and joy by the churches.

It's therefore not clear whether the Emperor's involvement with the Church was the result of genuine faith, or clever *Realpolitik,* or both (7). He might have seen increasing numbers of military defections to a pacifist faith as a threat to the efficiency and morale of the Imperial army. Stark and other scholars also suggest that the growth of the Church had been so rapid that Christians may even have been a majority in the Empire by the end of the 3rd century (4)(7). If that was indeed the case, Constantine's interest may in part have been his response to a demographic reality. If half his subjects were now Christian, he had better do something about it. So he took the 'if you can't beat 'em, join 'em' (and *then* try to change 'em) option.

Whatever his motives, which were almost certainly mixed at best, he made what amounted to a successful takeover bid by the Roman State for the Church, starting with an invitation to all the bishops within the Empire to attend a Council in Nicaea, in 325. Several hundred came, and he orchestrated the proceedings himself, with diplomacy and tact and also in some style. The main outcome of the Council was to draw the church from the periphery of Roman life to its centre, and in such a way that eventually it became part of the State, a merger which is discussed in more detail in the next chapter. The bishops, who had never previously met together in this way, clearly succumbed collectively to the political wiles of the Emperor, but they also took the opportunity presented by the Council to address issues of doctrinal uniformity. Work was started on the Nicene Creed, although it took a further 60 years for it to be finalised. Heresy inevitably became a major issue, and several attending bishops were excommunicated by the Council for this reason. Constantine, in perhaps the first official example of secular/ecclesiastical cooperation, promptly had these 'heretics' banished from the Empire.

The Violent Church

Nonviolence Abandoned

A cascade of short-reigning emperors after Constantine
was largely a consequence of the breaking up of the Empire
in the second half of the 4th century. Julian (361–363), who
reigned for 18 months before dying in battle, tried to stem the
relentless tide of 'Christianisation' of the Empire following the
Council of Nicaea, and attempted to reassert the primacy of
paganism. He failed. Eventually, in 380 it fell to Theodosius 1
(the 13th emperor since Constantine) to decree that Nicene
Christianity was henceforth to be the official religion of the
Roman Empire (9). Further edicts, banning all other religions,
led to the eventual elimination of all the pagan rituals, latterly
including worship of the Emperor himself, which had been
part of Roman daily life and culture for centuries.

The repercussions were far-reaching and profound,
as political and constitutional issues bit deeply into the
spirituality of the Early Church. The uncompromising wording
of the 380 Edict made the Nicene Creed Imperial law: it also
denounced non-believers as heretics, an epithet which has
cast a long and malevolent shadow down the centuries ever
since. It soon became clear the extent to which intolerance

and the rhetoric of violence had taken hold of the Church as a direct consequence of its merger with the State. According to the Edict, non-believers were deemed to be 'foolish madmen', to be chastised by divine condemnation and to receive 'the punishment of our authority which in accordance with the will of heaven we shall decide to inflict' (presumably that was the Imperial 'we') (9). Christians must have assumed that they had also been given at least implicit sanction to use violence themselves, and destructive internecine conflicts within the Church became commonplace (7).

The suppression of paganism was inevitably slow and met considerable resistance. After vain pleas by its supporters for tolerance, there was violence as temples and shrines were destroyed and pagan religious practices suppressed. The Church, as the newly constituted state religion, found itself historically in a role reversal, now being permitted – even encouraged – to use violence against its erstwhile persecutors. Nonviolence as a principled position had been thrown out of the proverbial church window.

Christendom

The Early Church had been centred on faith in the risen Lord Jesus, with an emphasis upon personal discipleship. Membership was through voluntary believer's baptism. The focus on the person of Jesus diminished following Constantine's 4th century interventions, and became even more blurred with the emergence thereafter of Christendom, the official amalgamation of Church and State. The Church itself underwent multifaceted changes, often referred to as the 'Christendom shift' (6), to reshape it for what was henceforward to be required of it; and the cumulative effects over time were momentous, even though some of the reshaping was quite gradual. Much of the remodelling can be attributed to Augustine's influence and advice (see pp 38–39).

The main practical outcomes were that:

- The Church, in becoming the official religion of the Roman Empire, moved from the edge to the centre of society. Membership became compulsory, eventually through infant baptism, at which stage adult baptism was banned. All citizens (except Jews), and all infants once baptised, were deemed to be Christians. Personal faith became irrelevant.

- Orthodoxy, the set of beliefs to be shared by all, was imposed by powerful church leaders with state support, and was defended from heresy, immorality and schism by legal sanctions up to and including the death penalty.

- A specifically 'Christian' culture was created and developed, covering all aspects of human life.

- A 'Christian' morality was imposed by legislation and custom. This became noticeably Old Testament in tone and content.

- Jesus, whose teaching and personal example during his ministry fitted very uneasily into much of what the Church now practised, was marginalised, and became a divine, celestial and haloed figure, often represented in art as sitting on a throne on high, at the right hand of God the Father and Judge. It is striking that the well-known creeds, formulated during this post-Early Church period, all skip straight from Jesus' incarnation and birth to his death, resurrection and ascension, as though his intervening life and ministry were of no consequence.

- The cross became a symbol to go on shields in battle, rather than representing the sacrificial love at the centre of Christian faith.
- The Church was organised on a hierarchical model of diocese and parish, which mirrored the structure of the civic authorities and was buttressed by the State.
- The known world was subdivided into Christendom and 'heathendom'. Wars were waged against heathendom in the name of Christ and of the Church. Political and military force was used to impose Christianity, and missionary outreach was much more likely to be with the sword than with the bible.
- These changes were justified biblically by reference to the Old Testament rather than the New.

The difference between matters ecclesiastical and secular often became so blurred within Christendom that distinctions disappeared. Here are a few examples:

- Odo, half-brother of William the Conqueror, was both Bishop of Bayeux and a military castle designer for the king.
- The concept of warrior bishops was widely recognised

and even admired in the Middle Ages, particularly around the time of the crusades.

- The deadly spat between Henry II and Thomas à Becket arose out of the archbishop's refusal to play secular politics the king's way.
- One of the French men-at-arms killed at the Battle of Agincourt in 1415 was an archbishop.
- In the early 16th century, Pope Julius II, who modelled himself on Julius Caesar, led his own army in battles.
- In Tudor England, the political shenanigans of the 16th century were claimed by all sides to be a matter of defending The Faith, whether Catholic (with undercurrents of foreign takeovers) or Protestant. Henry VIII, and his successors up to the present Queen, became head of the Church in England (but not in Wales, Scotland or Northern Ireland) instead of the Pope.
- In 17th-century France, Duc-Cardinal Richelieu was also a government minister, and had complex and sometimes conflicting loyalties to the Pope and the French King.
- In the early 18th century, Peter the Great of Russia abolished the Patriarchy of Moscow (the Patriarch had been the traditional head of the Russian church), and effectively turned the Russian Orthodox Church into a government department.

- Numbers of the princes and counts in the Habsburg Empire were also prelates. One such in the 18th century was Count Hieronymus Colloredo, Archbishop of Salzburg, who employed the young Mozart as both Court and Church composer, although a strict divide between Church and secular music was insisted upon.

With the emergence of Christendom, any religious freedoms there may have been in the Early Church disappeared. For the conforming citizen who was Christian by birth and compulsory baptism in infancy, all was well so long as he/she toed the Church line. If she/he did not do so, however, for any reason other than being Jewish, penalties were extreme. For example, those who were inquisitive about their faith risked being deemed heretics, and could then expect to be excommunicated, tortured or burned at the stake, or quite possibly all three, unless they recanted back to their unquestioning spiritual status quo. During the 6th century, re-baptism after infancy became a capital offence, and anyone publicly criticising infant baptism was liable to summary execution without trial.

Christendom had to weather many storms in its subsequent turbulent history. The collapse of the Western Roman Empire in the 4th and 5th centuries, the rise of Islam in the 7th, the Great Schism (with the Orthodox Churches) in the 11th, the fall of Byzantium in the 15th, the Reformation and Counter-Reformation in the 16th and the impact of the Enlightenment in the 18th century, were some of the biggest. To this list should be added four devastating pandemics, in the 2nd, 3rd, 6th and 14th centuries. The third of these mainly impacted the

Byzantine Empire; the fourth was, of course, the Black Death in Europe.

Churches within Christendom found themselves having to live and work with their state counterparts in a wide range of 'partnerships' across Western Europe. Some of these didn't work at all well (10). The various churches – the Roman Catholic and Eastern Orthodox Churches, and numerous Protestant Churches from the 16th century onwards – waxed and waned in power and influence relative to state partners, but almost invariably became actively involved in the violence which accompanied the rise and fall of individual nations.

It's fairly clear, however, that the concept of Christendom – in practice an ever-changing kaleidoscope of relationships between Popes and Potentates across Europe – did provide a degree of continuity, and even sometimes of stability, throughout the Middle Ages, while the rise and fall of nations and monarchies, political intrigues, marriages of dynastic and diplomatic importance, and the almost continuous marching to and fro of armies (with famine, starvation and epidemic diseases in their wake), swirled and eddied round it like rough seas round a lighthouse.

Perhaps surprisingly, the perceived need for Church and State to embrace, or at least cling on to, each other largely survived the Reformation. Those parts of Europe which became Protestant dispensed with the Pope, and radically revised their theology. A particular, indeed unique, variant of 'reformed' Christendom took root in 16th century England when Henry VIII made himself Head of the Church so that he could divorce his first wife – in the circumstances a purely political motivation. This particular entanglement of Church and State continues, and involves the British monarchy as it applies to England, to this day.

Augustine

In Murray's words, 'If Constantine laid the foundations of Christendom, its main architect was Augustine' (7). This was Augustine of Hippo (11), the outstanding theologian and ethicist of his time, who wrote prolifically and had a pervasive influence on the development of the Christendom system. (Please note that the aspects of his thought which are outlined very briefly here are confined to those related to the origins of church violence. As such, they do not even begin to provide anything like a balanced overview of his contribution to early Christian theology and ethics.)

- In order to move away from the pacifist stance of the pre-Constantine Church, official sanction for the use of force was required. Augustine used the concept of the 'just war', traceable back to the Egyptians and debated by the Greeks, to provide a Christian apologetic for this purpose. 'Just war theory' has dominated Christian thinking about warfare ever since (see pp 77–82 for further discussion). Christian soldiers were urged by Augustine to 'love' the enemies they killed.
- He 'developed an approach to biblical interpretation that enabled him to relate biblical teaching to the realities of Christendom, justifying from the Old

Testament practices he could not easily identify with the New' (7). He drew parallels between Israel and Christendom, claiming that Old Testament prophecies foretold a Christian empire; and he found Old Testament support for 'just war theory' in terms of defending such a realm. He also forged historically and theologically misguided links between circumcision and baptism, and around the reintroduction of the Jewish practice of tithing.

- Augustine propounded and developed the principle of *error non habit jus* (error has no rights) which the Church subsequently made the basis of its imposition of 'truth' on others.

- Coercion (the use of force or threats to persuade) became a pervasive tool for imposing 'truth'. Augustine sanctioned its use by the Church, initially, it must be said, with some reluctance, partly by placing excessive emphasis on a text in Luke's gospel, 'Compel them to come in' (Luke 14.23). The consequences, in terms of torture and gratuitous violence through the following centuries, have been terrible.

Decline and Fall

The Roman Empire disintegrated during the 4th and 5th centuries, and eventually broke into two. The eastern provinces remained relatively stable, and eventually became the Byzantine Empire, centred on Constantinople (see below).

The western Empire was invaded by waves of Germanic

warrior tribes and this area of Europe remained unstable for more than four centuries after the 4th. Relatively weak new kingdoms arose and then fell apart in short order, to be reconfigured again before further dissolution. Some of the warlords and would-be monarchs caught up in these ructions were already 'Christians'; others, particularly those further north, remained pagan for centuries. Conversion to Christianity and coercion remained closely intertwined far beyond the fall of the Roman Empire. Charlemagne, for example, crowned by the Pope as the first 'Holy Roman Emperor' in 800, used to follow up his conquests of pagan kingdoms by offering his new subjects the binary choice of conversion to Christianity or execution. On one campaign he personally supervised the massacre of over 4,000 recalcitrant Saxon prisoners-of-war (7).

Byzantium

Apart from some passing references and this brief summary, quite a chunk of church history – that part relating to churches in the eastern half of the Roman Empire and its sequelae – has been omitted from this account. The eastern provinces became Byzantium, which was Greek-orientated in language and culture and centred on Constantinople. It grew to become the richest and most influential Empire in the eastern Mediterranean, probably because of its wealthy cities, powerful state apparatus and centralised church. However, it collapsed, relatively suddenly and completely, when Constantinople was sacked by the Ottoman Turks in 1453.

Self-styled 'Orthodoxy' survived, albeit with some

fragmentation, and became differentiated from Roman Catholicism, particularly after the Patriarch of Constantinople was excommunicated by the Pope in 1054 (The 'Great Schism'). (To confuse the issue of demarcation, a few small ancient churches with 'orthodox' in their titles have remained in communion with the Rome-based Catholic Church.) Orthodox churches were as prone to infighting as the Roman Catholics and, after the Reformation, the Protestants, and they also waged war with 'heathendom'. Their collective views on the concept of holy wars, and on custodianship of Jerusalem and other sacred places in Palestine, differed from those of the Roman Catholic Church, and they did not contribute to the holy wars (crusades). However, they became entangled in the 13th-century Northern Crusades, targeted primarily against pagan Baltic peoples; and Byzantine and Teutonic knights found themselves fighting each other on occasion, for example in the 'Battle on the Ice' in 1242. Church and State have tended to be close in Russia – Peter the Great made the Russian Orthodox Church into a government department – except during the Soviet era. The nature of the Church-state relationship in Russia today is not entirely clear (but see p 46).

The Orthodox Churches have become theologically, liturgically and organisationally distinct from Roman Catholicism and Protestantism, and to some extent differ among themselves. It would be true to say that they are not well understood in Western Europe.

The Reformation

The principal reformers initially wanted to change the existing (Roman Catholic) Church rather than set up in opposition. When new Churches emerged notwithstanding, major features of Christendom were carried over into the new structures, including hierarchical ecclesiastical systems, maintenance of close bonds between church and state, continuing infant baptism, and, at least in theory, application of just war rules to issues of fighting (see p 38 and pp 77–82). Martin Luther supported the right of the protestant nobility to rule autocratically, and they in turn supported him.

The Protestant Churches proved, in practice, to have little interest in improved social justice. This was starkly illustrated by the Lutheran reaction to the so-called Peasants' War in 1524–25. Several uprisings of peasantry coalesced, and their leaders invoked divine law to demand improved agrarian rights and freedom from tyrannical nobles and oppressive landlords. They looked to Luther for support, and at first, he was sympathetic, at least to some of their grievances. In 1525, however, his attitude changed, and in his polemic *Against the Robbing, Murderous Hordes of Peasants* he encouraged the nobles to oppose the rebels with extreme violence. They must, he wrote, be 'sliced, choked, stabbed, secretly and publicly, by those who can [do so], like one must kill a rabid dog'. The aristocracy obliged by putting down the uprising, with such savagery that about a 100,000 mostly unarmed peasants were slaughtered.

Religious Wars

Definitions of wars of religion, or of wars as 'religious', are problematic because the causes of war are usually complex. A great deal of mostly religion-inspired fighting took place in Europe between 400 and 1100, and thereafter at least 39 conflicts between the 12th and 18th centuries can reasonably be called wars of religion (12). Here are very brief thumbnail sketches of some of them, to illustrate the extent of the violence for which the Church was directly or indirectly responsible, and some of the consequences.

- Crusades were 'holy wars' (not actually called crusades until centuries later), called for by a succession of Popes in the Latin Church during the mediaeval period. The best known are the seven principal expeditions to the Holy Land between 1096 and 1291. The first Crusade eventually conquered Jerusalem, after a siege which was followed by a merciless and bloody *two-day* massacre of the inhabitants, Jewish and Muslim, who had allegedly been given solemn assurances by the crusaders about their safety. Overall, the Crusades to the Holy Land failed, and Muslim control of Jerusalem was re-established in the late 13th century. The crusading armies generally behaved badly, ransacking and pillaging their way across Europe and Asia Minor, and especially attacking and massacring Jews. The later 13th-century Northern Crusades aimed to convert by force – not by missionary outreach – the remaining pagan areas of northern Europe, and also fought Eastern Orthodox Christians.

- The Hussite Wars (1419–1434) in Bohemia and Moravia followed the burning at the stake of Jan Huss in 1415. He was one of the earliest Protestant reformers, and was accused of heresy. The Hussites defeated five consecutive Crusades ordered against them by the Pope.

- The Protestant Conquest of Catholic Ireland was undertaken messily by the Tudor monarchs and their Protestant allies (1529–1603); and brutally by Royalist, Parliamentarian and Scottish Covenanter forces in the Irish Confederate Wars (1641–1652).

- The French Wars of Religion (1562–1598) were major consequences of the influx of Protestant ideas into France following the Reformation. During the wars and popular unrest which followed, three million people are estimated to have died from combat, disease and famine. Fighting was between Catholics and Protestants (Huguenots), with a complex international back story involving the French Succession. Seven fairly discrete periods of war are generally recognised over a 30-year period. The St Bartholomew's Day Massacre took place between the third and fourth wars: some 5,000 to 30,000 Huguenots were slaughtered (historical estimates vary), initially in Paris and subsequently throughout the country. The Edict of Nantes in 1598 finally brought most of the fighting to an end.

- The Eighty Years' War (1568–1648) was a protracted Protestant–Catholic conflict, mainly between the Netherlands and Spain.

- The Thirty Years' War (1618–1648) erupted when the King of Bohemia (who later became Holy Roman Emperor) attempted to impose Catholicism throughout his dominions, and Protestant nobles rebelled. By the 1630s most of Europe was embroiled, and it is estimated that by 1648 eight million people had died as a result of the war, from a combination of violence, famine and disease. The suffering endured by ordinary people was terrible (13), and the conflict is widely regarded as having been the most destructive European war prior to WW1.

- The English Civil Wars (1642–1651). The underlying religious tension was fear of a resurgent Roman Catholicism in Protestant Stuart England. In the second war, the soldiers in Parliament's New Model Army were each issued with a 'Souldiers Pocket Bible' as an item of their military equipment.

- The Williamite War in the North of Ireland (1688–1691) followed the Glorious Revolution in 1688, which deposed Catholic James II and replaced him with Protestant William III of Orange, and Mary. James attempted a comeback in the north of Ireland with the support of Irish Catholics, but was defeated by William. This war and its religious background and consequences sowed the seed of the sectarian violence which erupted as the 'Troubles' in Ulster between 1969 and 1998, as a result of which 3,600 people lost their lives.

- With the Enlightenment's banishment of God (see pp 62–64), the concept of religious wars petered out into the vaguer idea of 'sectarian conflicts'. Wars of religion have not completely disappeared, however, and in more recent times:

- Lebanon. During the civil war in the 1980s, members of Christian militias celebrated the Eucharist each morning, and then set out on killing sprees, bragging rights being claimed in the evening by those who had killed the greatest number of Muslims during that day (14).

- Russia/Ukraine (2014 and ongoing). In 2018 the Orthodox Churches in Russia and Ukraine declared themselves to be in schism with each other over the military tensions between their two countries (15), which were simmering then and have boiled over in 2022. Warnings at that time that 'blood will be spilt' have proved to be horrifyingly prescient. An editorial in *The Observer* newspaper on 6 January 2019 commented, rather remarkably, that 'the conflict is partly about who blesses the guns of which army, but since that is a question that affects a soldier's willingness to fight, and die, it matters to millions who have no interest in theology' (16). Russian Patriarch Kirill has declared that Vladimir Putin has been 'sent from God'. In April 2022 he blessed a large assembly of young Russian conscripts gathered in something called a military cathedral, declared that the conflict in Ukraine was a 'holy war', and told them to go and do God's bidding in Ukraine.

Civilians and War

Non-combatants have always been collateral damage in times of war, and famine and disease which accompany any periods of prolonged fighting also take a terrible toll particularly in impoverished countries, for example in Yemen, Eritrea and Afghanistan in 2021. Furthermore, atrocities committed by troops in wartime often target civilians, as happened, for example, during the crusades, in the Thirty Years' War, and recently in the Balkans and in Ukraine. However, war *strategies* which deliberately include attacks on civilian populations are, historically speaking, a relatively recent development. Early examples were French accusations that Germany targeted civilians with artillery in Alsace during the 1870 Franco-Prussian War; and bombing raids, using both airships and aircraft, on mainland Britain during WW1, which killed over 1,500 people between 1915 and 1918, and caused fear and outrage because the intended targets were non-combatants.

In 1937 German dive-bombers attacked Guernica on General Franco's behalf during the Spanish Civil War, killing thousands. Also in 1937, during the second Sino-Japanese War, Nanking was bombed and many inhabitants were massacred. It seemed that a new and horrible kind of warfare had arrived and, well before the USA's entry into the impending world war, US President Theodore Roosevelt was provoked into appealing to all governments. 'The bombing of helpless and unprotected civilians is a strategy which has aroused the horror of all mankind'; and he urged that this inhuman practice be prohibited. *Less than five years later*, in response to German bombing of cities such as London and Coventry, Winston Churchill spoke of beating the life out of Germany. The fire-bombing of Dresden, which was packed with refugees from air raids elsewhere and of little strategic significance, presumably demonstrated what he meant. In 1945, *a mere eight years after Guernica, the first atomic bomb was dropped on Japan.* US President Harry Truman, once described as an outstanding Baptist layman and now standing on the deck of a US battle cruiser as the second bomb was dropped on Nagasaki, is said to have exclaimed, 'This is the greatest thing in history!' (17), forgetting or ignoring the day some 19 centuries previously which really had been the 'Greatest Thing'. Most American Christians, at that time and since, have supported their Presidents in actual and potential use of nuclear weapons, thereby giving tacit consent to, and complicity in, a new and monstrous moral evil.

Since the Cold War, and with complete international failure to control the spread of nuclear weapons, it now seems that only the strategy of MAD (= 'Mutually Assured Destruction'; *please just pause to take in the ghastly aptness of that acronym*) is keeping one or both or all sides from reducing the world to an uninhabitable wilderness following a nuclear holocaust. Is that a deafening silence I hear from churches almost everywhere?

Since March 2022, even with nuclear, chemical or biological weapons not yet factored into the equation of the developing Ukraine war, the deliberate targeting of non-combatants is clearly becoming a military norm for some.

Atrocities

In October 2017 in the UK, prior to the annual Guy Fawkes commemorations in November, a vivid TV drama-documentary examined the background to the Gunpowder Plot in 1605. Historians reconstructed the sort of events, typical of the period, which might have contributed to what took place. The opening scene was a quiet, tense, malevolent manhunt in a domestic setting, during which two arrests were made. The view then switched to a noisy crowd, in front of which a young man was – very realistically – hung and drawn; viewers were spared the quartering. A middle-aged woman was then required to strip naked, again in public, before she was crushed to death. The pair were mother and son: he was training for the Catholic priesthood. Their 'crime' was that they were Roman Catholics in Protestant Stuart England.

Man's inhumanity to man, and the devilishly cruel ways it's been practised, is nearly as old as mankind itself – one dismal manifestation of the 'fall', the fault line in creation. The earliest Church was frequently on the receiving end of atrocities perpetrated by Rome, often for the entertainment of the public. (Martyrdoms, of course, continue to the present day; Christians are still being tortured and killed because of their faith in Jesus.) When Christendom took to combating heresy with force and trying to compel people to believe specific doctrines, they didn't need to invent any of the means: these were ready to hand as part of the close relationship between Church and State.

The burning of heretics, the various inquisitions set up by

the Catholic Church, and the reputation of some monastic orders for obtaining confessions and conversions by means of torture are all well documented examples of the many atrocities perpetrated by the Church. Their work speaks louder than my words, and detailed analysis would be unnecessarily harrowing. However, two points should be remembered. First, these horrors were often committed *specifically in the name of faith in Jesus.* Second, after the Reformation this religious barbarism was practised on a busy two-way street, early Protestant torturers showing at least as much zeal in their work as those in the Roman Catholic Church. Catholics, incidentally, tended to be beheaded or hanged, drawn and quartered, whereas Protestants were usually burned at the stake. Catholics and Protestants did however share common cause in trying to root out and exterminate Anabaptists, who advocated consenting adult baptism and nonviolence.

Religious atrocities did not die out with the passing of the Middle Ages, as even a cursory look at the history summarised above shows. There have been sectarian drownings and slaughterings of women and children in Ireland (15th–16th centuries); mass murders of Protestants in France (16th century); appalling suffering of civilians during religious wars throughout central Europe (16th century); the 20th-century Troubles in Ulster, erupting from the deep-seated festerings of a religious war 250 years earlier; anti-Jewish pogroms organised by the Church in Imperial Russia (23); mutilation of Muslim corpses and graves by Christians in Lebanon's civil war (14) (20th century); and the torture and/or lynching of nearly

4,000 black people in the Southern United States between 1850 and 1950 (18), some incidents being celebrated in an overtly 'Christian' context – of 'white', good and Godly triumphing over 'black', satanic and evil. It is little wonder that the 18th-century 'men of reason' tried, although they manifestly failed (see p 63), to find ways to bypass the evil in human hearts.

Anti-Semitism

The history of the Jews has been summarised as 'a story of external dispersion and internal cohesion' (19). At the time of Jesus' ministry, Jews living in Palestine were probably outnumbered by those scattered throughout the Roman world, including large Jewish communities in centres of population such as Rome, Antioch and Alexandria. Taken together, Jews may at times have accounted for as much as 10 per cent of the Empire's population. Following the destruction of the Temple – the epicentre of Judaism – in 70 AD, and the crushing of the Bar Kokhba revolt in 135, thousands of Jews were captured and removed from Palestine, many being sold into slavery. This final diaspora was carried out with characteristic Roman ruthlessness.

Jesus had addressed his own ministry almost exclusively to the Jews, but his final Great Commission after his resurrection (Mat 28.19–20) embraced 'all nations'. Peter's encounter with Cornelius (Acts 10.1-48), which was clearly prompted by the Holy Spirit, suddenly widened the scope of apostolic outreach to include non-Jews, and Acts and Paul's letters give some idea of the seismic change in attitudes and practices this demanded of the Jewish founders of the Christian faith (20). In the 50s poverty experienced by the church in Jerusalem was made worse by famine and Jewish in-fighting (Acts 11.29–30), and ironically it was the increasingly Gentile and relatively wealthy wider church which provided some relief for their Jewish Christian brethren at this time (Rom 15.25–28). After the destruction of the Temple in 70 AD, the remnant church in and around Jerusalem may have continued to combine Christian and Judaic practices for a while, until remaining vestiges of Judaism there were eventually stamped out by Rome.

The majority of Jews refused to recognise who Jesus was and what he came to do. It is nevertheless sad how relatively soon most of the early churches came to lose touch with their Jewish origins. Political reverberations from the Jewish-Roman wars in 66–70, 115–117 and 132–136 may have made it difficult for the Gentile churches to associate too closely with Jewish Christians. Ponsonby thinks that none of the bishops who attended the Council of Nicaea in 325 came from a Jewish background (21). One of the outcomes of that Council was to switch calculation of the date of Easter each year from the Jewish to the Julian calendar: this severed what may have been the last official link between the Church and its Judaic roots.

Judaism survived the destruction of the Temple and the dispersal of Jews throughout the Mediterranean world, and beyond, by means of a focus on pharisaic and rabbinic teaching, the codification of the 'oral Torah', and spiritual and communal life centred on synagogues. There was a certain amount of scholarly interaction with the Early Church, notably with Origen in Alexandria where there was a large Jewish community. In general, however, Christendom came to regard Jews with increasing hostility, which was reciprocated. Jewry was held responsible for the death of Jesus (Mat 27.25), and Jews were persecuted for their alleged involvement in fabricated atrocities such as the 'blood libel' (there is nothing new about fake news). An increasingly extreme anti-Semitic literature emerged from the time of the early Church Fathers, and was added to by the Catholic Church and, later, by leading Protestant reformers, including Martin Luther in his final years. (It should be added that equally vitriolic anti-Christian propaganda can be found in the Talmud (22).)

Over the centuries, anti-Semitism erupted from time to time in the form of extreme physical violence against Jews. Much of it was initiated by the Church, but at clergy level rather than by more senior members of the hierarchy; the Holocaust was, of course, the most notable 'non-Church' exception. The following incidents are a very small selection of those on record:

- The expulsion, by Constantine, of Jews from Rome (325)
- The Rhineland massacres (1096) preceding the First Crusade
- Atrocities targeting the Jewish communities in the Holy Land during the crusades (1097–1293)
- The expulsion of Jews from England (1290)
- Massacres of Spanish Jews (1391)
- The Spanish Inquisition (from 1478)
- The expulsion of Jews from Spain (1492)

- Cossack massacres of Jews in Ukraine (1648–57)
- Anti-Jewish pogroms in Imperial Russia (1821–1916) (see below)
- The Final Solution leading to the Holocaust (1938–1945) (see below)
- Soviet anti-Jewish policies (from 1945).

The Russian pogroms were frequent, often large-scale, targeted and *church-led*. Most took place on Feast Days of the Church – Easter was a favourite – and were fomented by clergy. A reporter from *The New York Times*, who witnessed what happened in Kishinev at Easter in 1903, wrote, 'The mob was led by priests, and the general cry "Kill the Jews" was taken up all over the city … The scenes of horror attending this massacre are beyond description. Babies were literally torn to pieces by the frenzied and bloodthirsty mob … At sunset the streets were piled with corpses and the wounded … the city is now practically deserted of Jews' (23). This awful event was sadly typical of many others during the final century before the revolution in Russia, and the revolution itself probably did nothing at all to improve the lives of Russian Jews.

The Final Solution in Hitler's Germany was the ultimate atrocity in terms of the scale and efficiency of the killing machine. However, according to Simon Ponsonby (21), '*every single edict of the Nazis against the Jews had a precedent in earlier decrees by the church*' (emphasis mine). It was no coincidence that Kristallnacht in 1938, which kicked off the official anti-Semitic foment, took place on Martin Luther's birthday, which was celebrated every year throughout the Protestant parts of Germany, because National Socialism latched onto the extreme and extraordinary anti-Semitism of Luther's final years, and exploited it to the full. There was, however, one important difference between Church and Nazi anti-Semitism. The Nazis acted as they did because of some godless, vicious, crackpot theory of racial purity: the Church, when it persecuted and murdered Jews, *did so in the name of Jesus Christ.*

Stark (21) has pointed out that the Roman Catholic Church has never been 'officially' anti-Semitic. Indeed, several bishops in the Rhineland at the time of the first Holy War (crusade) tried unsuccessfully to protect Jews who were being killed by mobs; and Popes have spoken out from time to time against the persecution of Jews. The role and influence of Pope Pius XII during the Third Reich continues to be uncertain, and unfortunately is still researched and debated more at a sensational than intellectual level.

Most Protestant Churches in Germany, which had been centres of progressive theological thinking and the spiritual home of the intellectual giants of Protestantism during the late 19th and early 20th centuries, seem to have coped with Nazism either by looking the other way and pretending that nothing untoward was going on, or by adapting and assimilating National Socialist ideas, including its anti-Semitism, with varying degrees of enthusiasm and in order to avoid persecution by the state. A minority of influential Christians, including Martin Niemöller, Dietrich Bonhoeffer (41*), Hendrikus Berkhof (26) and Karl Barth, spoke out against what was happening, identifying themselves as the 'Confessing Church' in opposition to the Reichskirche. After the war it took some Protestant Churches in West Germany several decades to admit their guilt and express repentance for their involvement, largely by acquiescence, in the Holocaust (21).

Anti-Semitism was obviously not confined to Germany before WW2, and didn't simply shut down in war-torn Europe after 1945 – very far from it. As aid parcels began to arrive from outside Europe, mainly from the USA, some were marked 'Not for the Jews'. Intermittent persecution continued in many countries, particularly in the Soviet Union where it was largely hidden because it was undocumented. After more than a century of church-orchestrated anti-Semitism in Russia, followed by 60 years of Soviet oppression, 1.6 million Jews took the opportunity given to them to leave Russia between 1968 and 2006, the majority emigrating to Israel.

Perspectives

Before looking at some of the implications for Christians of my brief historical survey, I want to outline six concepts which I hope will provide useful background to discussion in later chapters. They are 1) worship and idolatry, 2) God's purposes in human history, 3) some implications of the 18th-century 'Enlightenment', 4) the Powers, 5) dissonance, 6) *agape* (Christian love).

Worship and Idolatry

God is love (1 John 4.16); it is his nature. Human beings have been made in his image, and disciples of Jesus are charged with taking on as much of the nature of God as they can. They are commanded to 'love God with all your heart … and love your neighbour' (Luke 10.27). They are also required to love their enemies, in a new dispensation which cancels the retributive aspects of the old law (Matt 5.44).

One of the most important ways humans show God that they love him is in worship (John 4.24), an activity which, whatever form it takes, helps to make each worshipper more like Jesus, and therefore more completely human.

The worship of anyone or anything other than God the

Creator himself is idolatry. This is an activity promoted by dark forces which work to thwart the divine plan, and in particular to attack and spoil man's relationship with God. The origin and nature of these forces, which are outside the scope of both Judaic and early Christian superstition, are looked at separately below (see – The Powers, p 64). They seem to be related to what tradition calls the fall; they were part of God's good creation, before being hijacked for destructive ends. Historically, Christians have usually identified the Powers with Satan or the devil, but they can also be discerned and experienced, no less vividly or destructively, as impersonal. They seem to be energised and resourced, directly or deviously (Luke 4.5–8), by human worship which should, according to divine purpose, be given to God. Collectively, they are the enemy who was *defeated* on Good Friday – it's worth hanging on to that – but they continue to instigate vicious rearguard actions in retreat, and engage us in constant spiritual warfare, even though their ultimate cause is already lost (24*).

According to John, for the moment 'the whole world lies under the power of the evil one' (1 John 5.19). Not at all a happy situation. We are told to beware idols, in all their guises, but also to thank God 'who gives us the victory through our Lord Jesus Christ' (1 Cor 15.57).

In our own times, it's both disconcerting and scary that all the old gods which have been worshipped through the ages – Mammon, Aphrodite, Mars, Bacchus – are very much alive, dressed up as money and status, unrestrained sex, power and violence and excessive consumption. Furthermore, they are busy recruiting new followers, with slick advertising campaigns to match. In today's post-Christendom world (see pp 122–125), we really do seem to be as beset by paganism and idolatry as the children of Israel were thousands of years ago, and as the Early Church was within the Roman Empire. Are we any good at discerning idolatry for what it is – and isn't – and resisting it?

God's Purposes in Human History

Like a zoom lens, the Bible gives us both the history of God's chosen people in close-up and his wide-angle purposes for all mankind, from creation right through to the early years of the Church; and of course, the post-Scriptures story continues through our own present and on into the future.

Tom Wright (25), among others, has suggested that imagining this meta-narrative as a cosmic drama can help us both to balance the Old and New Testaments, and also to work out what our own individual parts in the contemporary post-biblical story should be; because each of us does indeed have a part in the ongoing show.

The proposed five acts of this play are:

- Creation. God created everything, and it was, and is, very good (Gen 1.31). There is no dualism in the divine plan for creation. Humankind is created in the image of God (Gen 1.27), to worship him, to be his stewards of the created order and to reflect the praise and worship of creation back to its maker. In New Testament terms, they are to be a chosen people and his royal priesthood (1 Peter 2.9), in the new Temple which is the hearts and minds of all who worship him (1 Cor 3.16).

- The Fall. So that the bond between God and humans should not be one of no-choice slavery, man/woman was given the freedom to choose. And made the wrong choice. However it came about, the persisting result is a fault line of disobedience and distortion running right through creation, including through every single human being. It shows as, among other things, a tendency to indulge in power and violence, unrestrained sex, money and status and excessive food and drink (Col 3.5). As a consequence of the fall, unredeemed human nature constantly crashes its gears in its attempts to relate to the Creator God (Romans 7.19–20), as the other great world religions demonstrate.

- Israel. God moved to restore the divinely ordered status quo by setting up a unique Covenant with Abraham and his descendants. They would be his special people, and would be the channel *through which all nations of the earth* would be blessed (Gen 12.3; emphasis mine). However, from the golden calf incident onwards (Exod. 32 1–35), Israel, hemmed in by paganism on every side, succumbed repeatedly to the lure of idols as it struggled unsuccessfully to keep its side of the covenantal bargain. Idolatry became Israel's besetting sin, and turned Israel into part of the problem rather than its solution.

- Jesus. Second temple Judaism expected a Messiah to save and restore Israel. It did not anticipate the suffering servant (Isa 52.13–53.12), who taught peace and humility, and went to a shocking and ignominious death which became a triumph. Only after his resurrection and the gift of the Holy Spirit did his disciples start truly to understand who he was, what he had achieved, and its stupendous significance for them (Acts 2.36), and of course, for us.

- The Church. Act five is the history of the Church. Some scenes have, of course, already taken place. In the present and future, collective and *individual* (that's you and me) parts must be improvised, and they will contribute to the eventual climax of the whole story – which is, of course, the creation of a new Heaven and Earth under the lordship of Jesus.

Two further points are very important. First, the first four acts and early scenes of the fifth are already in the past, and obviously cannot be changed. We latter-day actors must therefore take care that our parts make sense in terms of what has gone before. Second, the improvisations required of all of us, now and in the future, are most emphatically *not* some kind of thespian free-for-all. The kind of dramatic spontaneity which is needed demands, paradoxically, paying constant close attention to what others around us are doing. This paradox is well recognised; ask any actor or musician who has worked without a script or score.

The Enlightenment

For most of the past two millennia in Western life and culture, the assumption that God both exists and also rules in the affairs of men was universal and largely unquestioned. Christian values were the gold standard, even when they were not actually achieved. Thinkers wrestled with problems of good and evil in terms of their effects upon *God's* world.

This *Zeitgeist* changed radically as a result of the so-called Enlightenment in the 18th century. It didn't happen overnight and was a complex phenomenon, but two important contributing influences were, first, the legacy of religious wars in the proceeding centuries (see pp 43–46) which caused immense suffering in the name of religion; and, second, the impact of natural disasters, often somewhat glibly referred to as 'acts of God' even today, especially the earthquake and tsunamis which devastated Lisbon in 1755, killing tens of thousands of people while they were attending to their religious obligations. These events had a profound effect on Europe's thinkers. What sort of God, they asked, could allow such things to happen? At best he must be capricious; at worst he is downright nasty.

Enlightenment thinking became pervasive. The concept of a God-in-charge was replaced by a personal-faith-only God who was metaphorically banished to a guest room in the attic of individual minds, or to ancient ecclesiastical buildings for a more collective experience, where those of a pious disposition could spend time with him if they so wished. Heaven, whatever that meant and if it existed at all, was definitely elsewhere. Men who considered themselves to be rational and enlightened took over running the affairs of society and the body politic, and religion became marginalised in public life. Science increasingly took over from what was regarded as superstition, creating an artificial rift between science and religion. Executive monarchies receded before a tide of democratic ideals such as *vox populi vox dei* ('the voice of the people is the voice of God'), and republics such as those of France, the United States and Soviet Russia devised constitutions specifically or implicitly excluding God as a guiding influence.

Enlightenment man was to be guided by rationalism and science. His modernism has now been replaced by postmodernism and beyond, characterised in general by broad scepticism, subjectivism, relativism and suspicion of reason. (I must say it sounds a bit unsure of itself. What next? I wonder.)

'You will know them by their fruit' (Mat 7.16). The outcomes, including imperialism and exploitation on a grand scale, two devastating world wars, Hiroshima, Nagasaki and the threat of nuclear annihilation, among many others, speak for themselves. Manifest evil has thrived in the forms of genocides, the Holocaust, gulags and the activities of Hitler, Stalin, Pol Pot and others. Rational people are also on the brink of destabilising our planet's precious and sensitive ecosystems, perhaps irreversibly.

We are said by some to be children of the Enlightenment. Certainly, its equivocal legacy has survived into the 21st century, greatly diminishing the potency of religion in both personal faith and public discourse. For many Christians, Emmanuel is 'God sort of with us, but not actually here'. Religion and politics mustn't mix, nor – according to the increasingly shrill and strangely ill-informed polemics of the Dawkins school – must religion and science.

The Powers

Paul made references to Powers which seem in some way distinct from, although often related to, the activities of the evil one. To the Ephesian Church he wrote, 'For we do not have to wrestle against flesh and blood, but against principalities and powers, against the world rulers of this darkness, against the evil spirits in heavenly places' (Eph 6.12). Again, but with somewhat different emphasis, he wrote to the Christians in Colossae, 'For in him are all things created, which are in heaven and on earth, the visible and the invisible, whether thrones, dominions, principalities, powers; all things are created through him and for him' (Col 1.6): and a chapter later, 'He disarmed the principalities and powers and made a public example of them, triumphing over them thereby' (Col 2.15). There are six other verses in Paul's letters which refer to the 'principalities and powers'. There is also one intriguing Old Testament reference to an incident involving troublesome powers, requiring the intervention of the Archangel Michael, no less (Dan 10.12–13).

Paul had trained as a strict pharisee, and would have been familiar with all strands of contemporary Jewish philosophical and theological thought. It was assumed until quite recently that the Powers verses probably related to some obscure themes in second temple apocalyptic thinking and writing. During and after WW2, however, theologians confronting fascism and, later, Soviet totalitarian regimes found strong resonances in Paul's Powers references with their contemporary predicaments. Hendrikus Berkhof, a Dutch theologian and a member of the Confessing Church during WW2, was one of the first to subject the Powers to academic scrutiny (26), followed by Yoder (27) and Wink (28). Walter Wink came to envisage the Powers as a matrix of influences and institutions, inherently not necessarily evil and some at least involved in the greater good. For example, we all benefit from social cohesion; we all need a fair justice system and human nature benefits from communities which support the individual's basic needs of nurture, security and love. However, some Powers, according to Wink, have been corrupted and taken over for evil purposes. He suggested that the emergence of the Mesopotamian conquest states around 3000 BC led to these negative Powers evolving into what he called the Domination System of today. This has, as its main characteristics, unjust economic relations, oppressive political relations, biased race relations, patriarchal gender relations and hierarchical power relations. Domination is imposed – men over women, masters over servants, priests over laity, aristocrats over peasants, rulers over people. And *violence*, he suggested, is the glue or mortar which binds all this injustice together.

In his book about the Powers in our daily lives (28), Wink also suggested that there is a myth of redemptive violence (a succinct and self-explanatory phrase) deeply embedded in the collective Western psyche. The second chapter of his book has the title 'The Domination System', and explores the extent to which this myth has legitimised the levels of violence absorbed by children from comics, TV and films. It's a plausible and terrifying read, the more so because it was published in 1998, *before* the internet and social media provided thick additional layers of gratuitous and often extreme violence which now threaten to smother the well-being of many young people. The third chapter, 'Jesus' Answer to Domination', is a blessed and much needed antidote. God protect our children! – because it seems that we can't – or won't.

In the real and modern world, conquest and exploitation by the mighty has largely given way to the idea of redemption through violence – that is to say, attempting to resolve differences by the use of force. It doesn't work but it's led, at international level, to interventionist foreign policies which need large permanent war machines to back them up; and these in turn must be fed by industries which create, make and market increasingly sophisticated weaponry with which to kill, maim and destroy.

If we are to make any impression on violence in human lives today, we need to recognise and try to understand the Powers and how they operate, and to confront them in the name of Jesus. This is a spiritual conflict which involves us all. Remember, the war is already won (1 Cor 15.57), but the rearguard skirmishes with a resourceful enemy certainly aren't. We must also remember that Jesus came not only to save us from the Powers, but also *to redeem the Powers from themselves,* so that they once again become part of God's plan for his creation.

Cognitive and Spiritual Dissonance

The psychological concept of dissonance has been mentioned already (see p 6). It is the means whereby a person attempts to hold two contradictory ideas simultaneously. The attempt to make conflicting notions consistent with each other may be psychologically stressful, and the clash between an individual's beliefs on the one hand and perceived new ideas on the other can be especially challenging. In order for an individual to cope, the opposites may have to be corralled from each other in the mind, mostly unconsciously, so that they can be experienced separately and in distinctly different circumstances, without colliding and thus triggering discomfort, or even dysfunction.

In retrospect, I'm sure that my teenage perplexity about the ethics of Corps at a Christian school (see Chapter 2) was a classic case of irreconcilable ideas being managed (by all concerned, staff and pupils alike) by compartmentalising them. Only then could we cope with incongruities such as 'love your enemy', *except* on Tuesday afternoons when we were encouraged to 'kill the enemy', and late on Friday mornings when we were urged to 'lob in a hand grenade'. Otherwise, we were encouraged to be truly Christian in ourselves and to each other.

In the wider and grown-up world, this dissonance – between the nonviolence which Jesus taught and practised, and general acquiescence in the world's violence – is as profoundly relevant today as it has ever been. Christians who choose not to confront it may be hoping to avoid or ignore the confusion/ambivalence/tension – call it what you will – which is, however, 'built in' and therefore inescapable. This particular clash of beliefs dates from the middle of the 4th century AD, an inevitable product of the union between the Roman State, which used violence and ruthless domination as its preferred means of conflict resolution, and the Early Church, faithfully embodying Jesus' nonviolent teaching and example (see pp 24–30). Humanly speaking, the resultant impasse could only be resolved the Roman way. Nonviolence was suppressed so that it did not interfere with the violent ambitions, first of Rome and then of Christendom.

We should be under no illusions, however. *God's* plan for his people and his Kingdom is grounded in his all-conquering, liberating, violence-free love for all of us. Think about it, because this particular spiritual/cognitive dissonance won't go away, and involves us all.

Agape (Christian Love)

Agape is a Greco-Christian word (first used as a noun in the Septuagint, the Greek translation of the Hebrew scriptures), which attempts to encapsulate God's unconditional love for humankind, and man's love of God in response. It is also used to delineate a love distinct from *eros* (erotic love) and *philia* (brotherly love). The human expression of *agape* is an unconditional love of neighbour and enemy, in obedience to God's commandments (Luke 10.27; Mat 5.44; Luke 6.27). As such, it is just as much a practical outworking as it is a spiritual experience or a sentimental feeling.

Agape is probably the best shorthand we have to indicate the type and quality of life within and around the Early Church.

It typified Christian interactions with fellow-Christians and pagans alike, and it astonished non-Christian observers (see pp 48–49).

The plural form, *agapai*, was used to describe communal meals, or love feasts (Jude 12), shared by members of the Early Churches. Such *agapai* are practised in some Brethren and Anabaptist communities to this day. The pagan Emperor Julian, commenting on the *agapai* of 'those impious Galileans', seemed to regard them as something between a food bank and a soup kitchen, but serving cakes! (37)

Taking Stock

What Went Wrong?

The earliest church, as described in Acts, lived out the teaching and example of Jesus. This was based initially on the first-hand accounts of those who had seen him, known him, heard him teach, misunderstood him, witnessed his death and post-resurrection appearances; and who had then been empowered by the gift of the Holy Spirit at Pentecost. This was the Gospel which the apostles and others took to Rome and the wider Empire.

There is no question that the spread of Christianity through the Roman Empire was astonishingly rapid during the first centuries of the Christian Era. Some scholars now think that by AD 350 there may have been as many as 35 *million* Christians in an Empire population of about 60 million (4). At the very least they had become a large and significant minority. The Roman historian Eusebius, who wrote a hagiographic *Life of Constantine*, suggested that it was the Emperor's conversion which stimulated the Church's rapid spread. However, it seems more likely that Constantine was responding to a demographic *fait accompli*, and that his conversion and involvement in Church affairs were results, rather than the cause, of that growth. Whatever his reasoning, he hijacked the Church, and he and his successors proceeded to make use of it in ways which suited them, with little reference to what the Gospel it had preached so successfully for more than three centuries was really about in the first place.

With the practices and ambitions of nascent Christendom making new demands (see pp 32–38), it probably became much harder for true disciples of Jesus to keep in touch with simple but essential truths within the Gospel, such as:

- Jesus on a hillside teaching about his Kingdom (Mat 5.1–7:27);
- Jesus demonstrating who 'my' neighbour is and what we should do about it (Luke 10.25–27);
- Jesus *taking up his cross, with all its consequences of suffering and death, and calling us, his disciples, to do likewise* (Luke 9.23);
- Jesus going to his death on our behalf, as nonviolently as a sacrificial lamb (Isa 53.7);
- the risen Jesus demonstrating, during a picnic breakfast on a seashore, how reconciliation and forgiveness work in practice (John 21.15–19).

Moreover, this Jesus-of-the-Gospels fitted so uneasily into the developing Christendom framework that he became increasingly misrepresented and marginalised in Church teaching (see pp 33–34 and 92–94).

Paul, writing at the end of the 1st century to the then tiny church in Rome, had described pagan society, there and elsewhere, in uncompromisingly negative terms (Romans

1.28–32). Now, no longer on the fringes and with the threat of persecution lifted, the Early Church was being coaxed into becoming part of that same society, whose paganism had probably changed little in the intervening years.

Murray (6) has discussed, in some detail, the likely inducements offered to individual Christians, and to the Church as a whole, to come on board with the Empire. They probably included special dispensations and enhanced status for the clergy, seats in high places for the bishops, and gifts of land and financial help with extensive building programmes to place basilicas in prominent positions in all major cities. Such sweeteners helped to make the Church highly visible in Roman society. For the ordinary Christian, the biggest carrot of all was undoubtedly the prospect of freedom of worship without fear of persecution.

The takeover of the Church can also be discerned in spiritual warfare terms. Peter had warned that 'Like a roaring lion, your adversary the devil prowls around, looking for someone to devour' (1 Peter 5.8). In a situation of change and likely uncertainty in the Church, the ever-lurking predator must have seen his chance, and pounced. It was a 'kill' of stupendous significance, Constantine and his successors having little if any idea of the extent to which they had been manipulated and exploited in the process.

The dark forces unleashed within the Church as a consequence – on the battlefield, subjugating heathendom, in the torture chamber, at the stake, persecuting heretics – have been summarised in Chapter 3. In later centuries, the tailing off of blatant savagery more or less coincided with the corresponding rise in influence of Enlightenment thinking in the 17th and 18th centuries (see pp 62–64). When Christendom's authority started to wane, the prince of darkness, having already house-trained the Church many centuries earlier to complicity in violence, could turn his attention to the 'enlightened' men-of-reason, who increasingly considered themselves to be in charge. Their subsequent dismal track record is summarised on p 30. Church involvement in violence having dwindled to little more than the compliance of good citizens, most Christians ever since then have been comfortable with the idea of military force being used on their behalf in circumstances deemed to be more or less 'just' (see pp 77–82). That outcome has, yet again, been a huge success for the dark prince.

Christians believe that God is working his purposes out, with or without our assistance. However, it could be that we collectively, far from being the help we fondly imagine, have repeatedly been a hindrance. In the five act play of spiritual history (see pp 59–61), Israel was to be the vehicle of God's redeeming purposes for mankind, but became part of the problem because of persistent idolatry. Humankind's shortcomings in Act 3 (Israel) were resolved only by Jesus' redemptive love in Act 4 (Jesus). There are uncomfortable parallels between Israel's failings in Act 3 and those of the Church in Act 5; and notwithstanding the relatively recent de-escalation of its in-house violence, the Church may indeed be getting in God's way in some respects. In the unfamiliar post-Christendom world we seem to be approaching (see pp 122–125)(4)), will the legacy of Christendom's past violence prove to be an obstacle to God's purposes in the present and future? Can we turn the page and start again with a clean sheet?

The Effects of Violence

Violence of any kind, whether between individuals, gangs, religious groups or nations, *always dehumanises*. Always. Every time. Without exception. (A reminder to rub it in – we are made in God's image; anything which dehumanises lessens that likeness.) From fists, cudgels and spears all the way through history to modern hi-tech combat, fighting degrades the combatants. The privations and horrors of war are brutalising (35*). Those training for war, and even training in peacetime for the possibility of war, are taught obedience-without-question in a chain of military command which ultimately makes human lives expendable numbers in pursuit of military objectives. Army recruits are taught 'bloody-mindedness'; practise bayonet drill or its modern equivalent and learn urban house-to-civilian-house fighting techniques (so much for protecting the vulnerable). For special forces, the requirement to dehumanise is greater still. In war zones, killed or wounded comrades provoke a desire for revenge, which motivates further fighting and killing. Air crew may find it somewhat easier to detach their emotions and better nature from the destruction they wreak, which usually happens at a distance with bombs and missiles. Similarly, warships now launch aircraft and missiles to streak off over the horizon, potentially inflicting remotely controlled 'shock and awe' havoc in the crowded streets of some far-off city. Drones and related technologies are now set to become the merciless, inhuman killing machines of the very near future.

In a major conflict, young lives are cut short, and more still are blighted by injury and ongoing disability. Historical shell shock (35*) has morphed into PTSD, which continues to wreck lives, relationships and families, and has been almost epidemic after some recent military campaigns. The economic cost is usually huge. The human cost – to individuals, families and communities – is incalculably high. Wars are feeding frenzy times for the prince of darkness and his minions.

The extent of collateral damage involving civilians is in direct proportion to their vulnerability. Women, the very young and very old, and those who are sick and disabled, are obviously most at risk. In wartime, ethical and moral norms are shelved: they have to be in order for it to become somehow acceptable, even if 'so very regrettable, alas', to inflict gratuitous violence on the defenceless.

Apologists for the need to think militarily contend that the end, of resolving whatever the dispute may be about, may justify the means – going to war – needed to resolve it. That argument is the myth of redemptive violence (see pp 64–66) writ large. History clearly shows, time after dismal time, the degree of self-deception involved in that sort of thinking. War never results in unambiguous and fair resolution of disputes, and it creates at least as many problems as it seems to solve. It causes avoidable death and injury, sometimes on a huge scale. In ultimately decisive military campaigns, it leaves a legacy of relative triumphalism on one side, humiliation and mistrust on the other, and deep scars in the personal and collective psyches of those involved. It damages infrastructure and the environment, wastefully and sometimes catastrophically. It degrades society.

The war in Ukraine in 2022, started with naked aggression of a kind probably not seen since 1938–45. It provides examples, if any more were needed, first, of the destructive futility of warfare as a means of conflict resolution; and second, of the sad fact that the one thing mankind learns from history is that it does not learn from history. Although not a war of religion, still less a 'holy war' (whatever the Russian Patriarch may say), in terms of the appalling suffering of ordinary folk this current conflict does evoke distant echoes of the worst religious conflict of all, the 17th century Thirty Years' War (see p 45).

All kinds of violence are now so much part of daily human life that we can easily forget how very destructive it is of us all as human beings. Those who have experienced actual combat in times of war, however, tend not to forget, or may be unable to do so. They are usually reluctant to talk about their experiences, probably assuming that we 'others' would find it difficult to understand their involvement in such barbaric behaviour (35*). Most of us only interact with extreme violence vicariously, voyeuristically, even unintentionally, in the switchable-off form offered by cinema, TV and computer games, all of which spare us some of the noise and all the smell, pain and wanton destruction of the real thing. Our behaviour raises the important question – *why* do we watch all this violence in the first place? There is no obvious answer. We do not seem able to resist, either individually or collectively.

Of course, it is true that many positive attributes of human nature – such as discipline, bravery, heroism, comradeship and self-sacrifice – can flourish in times of war. None of these saving graces, however, are peculiar to military contexts, and they cannot be used to justify violence. They can also be, thank God, healthy by-products of innumerable nonviolent, life-enhancing activities, including the work of emergency services, mountain, sea and cave rescue, and individual and collective responses to crises of all kinds; and even team sports!

Just War Theory

When the Church abandoned nonviolence under Constantine in the 4th century, it needed to find or devise both moral justification for fighting and killing, and also criteria allowing any warfare it became embroiled in to be assessed and, it was hoped, legitimised. St Augustine (of Hippo) obliged. Writing around 400 (see p 38), his was the most influential name in the early stages of formulating 'just war' thinking. The Popes who fomented holy wars (crusades) in the 11th to 14th centuries followed his lead. Eight centuries after Augustine, in the 13th century, when the so-called holy wars exposed inconsistencies (to put it mildly) in the Church's ethics related to fighting, Thomas Aquinas had a go at revising the Church's thinking about war, and just war theory continues to be tinkered with from time to time. It remains the Christian apologetic for violence (28) (30)(33)(34*), and is used by most Christian denominations to guide them, if they think they need guidance, and/or if Christian comment is sought or offered about potential or actual conflicts. It is even said to have influenced the drawing up and content of the Geneva Conventions.

Nevertheless, it has a very strange provenance. According to Murray (quoting John Howard Yoder) (7), 'it has never been promulgated by a council or a pope, never studied with great intensity, never formulated in a classical outline, and never applied with much consistency. It is dominant without being clear. It has taken over without being tested'. Wink referred to 'the infinitely malleable ideology of the just war' (28).

Lots of criteria have been put forward in attempts to justify war. They are usually divided into three categories, relating to before, during and after the fighting. Here are just a few of the many, with my added comments in italics.

Before the fighting starts ('*Jus ad bellum*') -

- Is the cause to be fought for just? *What is a 'cause' in this context? How is justness to be evaluated/quantified? How, and by whom, are opposing views of the justness of causes assessed?*

- Have all possible alternatives to fighting, such as diplomacy, been explored and exhausted? *Almost certainly not. There is always more time for talk to avoid fighting if those involved really want to avoid military action. They often don't.*

- Is war to be declared and fought by a legitimate authority? *How is one of those defined, and by whom? What, if any, are the consequences, to any side in a potential conflict, if one side is deemed, by whomever, not to be 'legitimate'?*

During the fighting (*'Jus in bello'*) -

- Is the conduct of the war itself just? *How is the conduct of a war in progress deemed to be just; or unjust?*

- Is the degree of military force being used proportionate? *Proportionate to what? Who decides? What happens if it is decided (by whom?) that disproportionate force is indeed being used?*

- Will all sides honour international accords on proscribed weapons – gas, chemical, biological etc. – and on the treatment of prisoners-of-war? *Probably not, especially if belligerents believe 'cheating' may give them a decisive military advantage. In WW1 gas was used, eventually by all sides. During WW2, both sides carried out extensive research into possible use of chemical and biological weapons. More recently, chemical and other proscribed weapons have been used in Syria. Since the 1930s, trends towards strategic targeting of civilians have been remorseless (see pp 47–48). In WW2 the International Red Cross exercised some control over the treatment of British, American, German and Italian prisoners-of-war; but none over German prisoners in the USSR and vice versa, nor over prisoners of the Japanese; in all these latter instances, treatment of PoWs was barbaric.*

- Are mechanisms in place for identifying and dealing with infringements and war crimes? *Nothing exists which is completely independent of the warring factions. Attempted use of structures such as the International Court in the Hague or the International Criminal Court has been hobbled by the refusal of the largest and potentially most belligerent nation states to recognise the Courts' jurisdictions.*

When the fighting stops (*'Jus post bellum'*) -

- Is there to be a just post-war diplomatic, political and humanitarian settlement and peace? *This category and criterion are relatively recent additions to just war theory. They post-date the WW1 armistice, and in any case would probably not have prevented the humiliation of Germany in the Treaty of Versailles (which was partly revenge for the ignominy experienced by France in and after the Franco-Prussian War in 1870), with all its disastrous longer-term consequences. No one would have been listening in the war-weary and retributive atmosphere at the time. More recently, where were the just post-war settlements following the Iraq wars? What will happen when the fighting in and around Syria finally stops? What about Yemen? And Eritrea? And Ukraine? In Afghanistan, serially invaded by Great Powers who have finally cut and run and have left the country facing humanitarian and political catastrophe, what would be, or could be, a truly just post-war settlement?*

Collectively these ideas are confused and confusing: and there's much more muddle around. Here are four of any number of further problems raised by just war theory.

First, it is detached from reality. Real life sadly does not provide teams of sober-minded, universally accepted and impartial umpires, who travel to potential or actual war zones to arbitrate calmly and with detachment on justness, proportionality and accusations of atrocities; or to make pronouncements to which any potential combatants would pay the slightest attention. It's never clear what is supposed to happen if just war criteria are not met. Do would-be combatants shake hands and go home? What about a Christian serving in the armed forces who does not like the 'justness credentials' of a particular potential conflict? Should he approach his commanding officer with, 'Sorry, sir, I don't like the look of what's coming. It's not sufficiently just from the point of view of my faith. Permission to miss out on this one, sir'? As I said, detached from reality.

Second, theoretical assessments cannot take adequately into account how human beings actually behave in situations *before* armed conflict – when feelings run high (otherwise war would not be under consideration); *during* armed conflict – literally in the heat of battle, when human behaviour becomes unpredictable and potentially savage (35*); and *after* armed conflict – when exhaustion, triumphalism and/or humiliation, resentment and revenge are likely to make rational appraisal and planning of the peace very difficult, if not impossible.

Third, just war theory, probably because it is indeed so airy-fairy, has never been applied with any rigour or consistency. If it had been, it would simply have collapsed under the strain of its unfitness for purpose. Nevertheless, the idea that war can be justified in these or similar ways continues to hover over any debate as a morally ill-defined and half-baked excuse for warfare. That simply isn't good enough. If the justness of any of the myriad wars in human history, recorded or forgotten, large or small, had been properly assessed using these criteria, virtually all would have been found wanting. Also, I doubt if a single conflict in human history has been called off by the would-be combatants because of just war deliberations. To put it no more strongly, that's a pathetic track record.

Fourth, and actually *overriding any other considerations*, just war theory seeks to justify fighting in certain circumstances. More than 16 centuries of obfuscation on this issue have muddied waters which should be crystal clear. In terms of nonviolence towards others, Jesus made no exceptions. Nor should we. For those of us who try to follow his teaching and example, just war theorising is simply and fundamentally a step too far, no matter what the circumstances may be.

Wink suggested (28) that it might help to create more common ground and dialogue if it were agreed to replace the term 'just war theory' with 'violence reduction criteria', and to start discussion again from there. I am not convinced.

Citizenship

Citizenship as a concept goes back to ancient civilisations. Aristotle held that citizens owed their primary loyalty to the state, not to themselves or their families, a view which has given the Greek, Roman and European Enlightenment philosophers much to talk about. During the Christendom era, de facto compulsory membership of the Church (see p 33), combined with the obligations built into the feudal system, required that the ordinary male citizen be prepared to lay down his life for the state, usually *via* his feudal lord; or for his faith, if that was a more effective propaganda line in particular circumstances. The historical, philosophical and psychological stage had therefore been well and truly set for many centuries before Field Marshal Douglas Haig, over a millennium later, poked his index finger out of early 20th-century posters, calling on young men to fight, and quite probably to die, in the WW1 trenches for the nebulous but powerful notion of 'King and Country'. Summoning people to put their lives on the line, fighting for a cause they may not understand or agree with, is a typical Domination System activity. Think, for example, of the men in their tens of thousands from far-flung colonised and exploited countries who were shipped to Europe to fight – and many to die – in the world wars, for reasons they could not possibly have properly understood.

From its early years, Christendom demanded absolute obedience and conformity from its citizens (see pp 33–34), with dire consequences for those who stepped out of line. It has taken a long time for the mighty State (in many, but by no means all, modern nation states) to start to allow people the basic right to opt out of fighting on grounds of conscience. To the extent that progress has been made in this respect, it's greatly to be welcomed.

Citizenship is something about which Christians have been brainwashed for centuries by the Christendom construct. In the special context of the Kingdom of God, both individually and collectively we should have clearly held and comprehensive beliefs which shape our actions (36*), and override any other considerations of allegiance. Do we? Are our beliefs that clear? See pp 128–130.

Women and Violence

Women have been closely linked to violence through the ages, in a relationship which, in terms of physical violence at least, is:

- almost entirely one way (they are victims);
- one of many blatant manifestations of the Domination System in action (see pp 64–66);
- an appalling consequence of unredeemed human nature.

I want to make four further brief comments about this huge, and hugely important, subject. The first is to underline a point already made, about the extreme vulnerability of women in times of war. They are almost always non-combatants, and – with menfolk often absent and fighting – are likely to be unsupported and without means to defend themselves. Their care of children, and often also care of the sick and very elderly, restricts the scope for them to run away, literally, from danger. War zones are increasingly often in densely populated urban areas where women and their dependents are congregated, and modern warfare no longer seems to know or care about protecting the vulnerable. We also have to put on record the age-old and appalling atrocity of rape as an instrument of war. It was ever thus, and shows no sign of abating.

Second, the vulnerability of women in modern society outside the violence of war has been brought into sharp focus in the past few years, perhaps particularly in the UK, by a series of high-profile unprovoked attacks which combined physical and sexual violence, and targeted women in circumstances where they should have felt and been absolutely safe, but clearly were not. There is a wide spectrum here, from unwanted physical/sexual advances from men in social and work environments – an aspect just beginning to receive the attention it deserves – to the rape and murder of women on their own, frequently at night. This is one aspect of male behaviour which *must* not be tolerated under any circumstances: but how can it be controlled? Here's a thought presumably being pondered – is easy and out-of-control access to pornography part of the problem?

Third, although there are exceptions, – for example, women in the armed services are increasingly involved in combat roles – inflicting physical injury is predominantly a male activity. It follows, remarkably but logically, that about half the population – the female half – is not usually directly involved in perpetrating *physical* violence on other people. Beyond the obvious reasons such as relative lack of muscular strength in women, we should ask ourselves why. Are there other contributory factors which make women less liable to be physically violent than men? If so, can we identify, acknowledge, celebrate and learn from them? Can any innate tendency to peaceableness in women – if that is indeed what it is – be made practical use of in, for example, reconciliation and mediation activities? It's unlikely to be quite as simple as that, unfortunately.

Fourth, sadly but inevitably, all women have their own fault lines related to the Fall (see p 60), just as all men do; and women contribute at least proportionally to verbal and emotional injury, and to Galtung's (29) categories of structural and cultural violence (see pp 90–92), in all of which gender distinctions do not apply.

Remembrance

(The following was a contribution to a recent primary school history project – 'The Armistice happened on November 11th in 1918, and every year since then we have had two minutes peace'.)

King George V introduced Remembrance Sunday in 1919, in acknowledgement and remembrance of the death toll in WW1 which had just ended. It has been celebrated annually since then, hoovering up remembrance of casualties in WW2 and other more recent major conflicts along the way. Equivalent events elsewhere include Veterans' Day in the USA, and Anzac Day in Australia and New Zealand. Officially these occasions are not intended to glorify war, and the mood is always appropriately sombre as a tribute to those who lost their lives. The fact that we in the UK were on the winning sides in both world wars makes it difficult to avoid a tinge of triumphalism, inevitably promoted in the tabloid press, at least for a few days in November each year. Presumably we try to remember and celebrate in a way which we hope gives dignity and value to individual sacrifices. Attempting to make them part of a worthwhile cause is not easy, however, when doing so flies in the face of the reasons for war, the stark reality of war, and the aftermath of war.

How can we anchor our remembrance in that reality? War footage films such as *They Shall Not Grow Old* will help to keep us honest in our recollections, if we can bring ourselves to watch bloated corpses floating in waist-deep mud, and direct hits by shells on horses pulling artillery ('*lots* of animals were harmed and killed in the making of this film'). *All Quiet on the Western Front* (35*) is a powerful anti-war novel which deserves to be read more widely and more often. Satire such as *Oh! What a Lovely War* still has a message. Contemporary films about more recent conflicts (WW2, Korea, Vietnam), with their focus on the gritty realism achievable with CGI, have at least lost some of the propaganda triumphalism of those from the earlier post-WW2 years. The battle scenes are horrifically realistic, but unfortunately these gory depictions of warfare, often shown on huge screens, have simply become part of the general diet of violence on which today's young people seem to feed (see pp 65–66).

War poetry can help us to remember, particularly when the emphasis is on the pointlessness of it all. Names such as Wilfred Owen, Siegfried Sassoon and Rupert Brooke are well known. Possibly less familiar is the writing of GA Studdert Kennedy (31), an Army chaplain, affectionately known as 'Woodbine Willie', who was a constant presence in the trenches throughout WW1. His vivid poems and doggerel verse reveal his struggles with faith and meaning in the context of war.

Folk songs have a directness which may address the futility

of fighting at least as evocatively as more formal war poetry. Here are extracts from the words of two ballads about WW1:

(Australian troops at Gallipoli)

> … And those that were left, well we tried to survive,
> In that mad world of blood, death and fire;
> And for ten weary weeks I kept myself alive,
> Though around me the corpses piled higher.
> Then a big Turkish shell knocked me arse over head,
> And when I woke up in me hospital bed
> And saw what it had done, well, I wished I was dead.
> Never knew there were worse things than dying.
>
> For I'll go no more waltzing Matilda
> All around the green bush far and free,
> To hump tent and pegs, a man needs both legs.
> No more waltzing Matilda for me.
>
> (from 'The band played waltzing Matilda')

(Sitting in a war cemetery in France, talking to the name on the nearest grave)

> … And I can't help but wonder, young Willie McBride,
> Do all those who lie here know why they have died?
> Did you really believe when they told you the 'cause'?
> Did you really believe that this war would end wars?
>
> Well, the suffering, the sorrow, the glory, the shame,
> The killing and dying it was all done in vain.
> 'Cos, Willie McBride, it all happened again,

And again, and again, and again, and again.

(from 'The Green Fields of France (No Man's Land)')

That is certainly what we should remember, and say – 'Never again!'

The Peace Pledge Union, a secular pacifist organisation in the UK, encourages wearing white poppies on Poppy Day to emphasise peace. It has also reminded us that

- in recent conflicts, *over 90 per cent of those killed have been civilians, mostly women and children.*
- the number of cadet forces in UK state schools has more than doubled since 2012 (see p 23 and p 89).
- the UK government has spent over £45 million on projects promoting a 'military ethos' in schools.
- Armed Forces Day is a new annual event since 2009.
- the UK is the only country in Europe to recruit 16-year-olds into the army.
- government documents leaked in 2017 reveal that targeting the poorest young people for recruitment is a deliberate strategy.

Of course we should remember. We should remember and mourn lost loved ones. We should remember and mourn the loss of so many innocent collateral-damage lives. We should remember and salute bravery. Above all, we should remember how destructively *pointless* it all was and is, and pray and work so that it doesn't happen again … and again … and again … and again … (as it seems to be doing once more in Ukraine in 2022).

A Wider View

Discussion of violence often gets no further than issues around armed conflict, but there's obviously very much more to it than that. In fact, taking stock of violence as a whole is very difficult because it's such a big, even amorphous, concept. To start with, how might we define it? Perhaps surprisingly, the short answer seems to be – with some difficulty. The Oxford Dictionary has a go, with 'behaviour involving physical force intended to hurt, damage, or kill someone or something': and also tries a legal definition of 'the unlawful exercise of physical force, or intimidation by the exhibition of such force'. The manifold inadequacies of both these definitions are remarkable. Among other deficiencies, they take no account of non-physical aspects, such as verbal violence which can be brutal; unspoken violent attitudes and psychological and emotional violence, including new concepts (but old realities) such as coercive control.

Johan Galtung, a sociologist with a long and distinguished academic career studying peace (and its absence) (29), has proposed a trifold paradigm of violence (30), with the aims first, of identifying three different types of violence – direct, structural and cultural; second, of examining how they interact and third of using these insights to look for and implement effective preventive strategies.

- **Direct violence** does not really require further definition. It is what we have been talking about.
- **Structural violence** refers to 'the physical, psychological and spiritual harm that certain groups of people experience as a result of the unequal

distribution of power and privilege … Structural violence degrades, dehumanises, damages and even kills people by limiting or preventing their access to the necessities of life'.

- **Cultural violence** is 'any aspect of a culture that can be used to legitimise violence in its direct or structural form'. (It would be difficult to come up with a more succinct definition of gun culture in the USA.)

Violence can be visualised as a kind of iceberg floating in the sea of society's presumably civilised behaviour, with direct violence visible above the surface and therefore usually getting most attention. Structural and cultural violence are the underwater parts which are more extensive, and can be just as destructive.

Here are two scenarios, taken from not infrequent real-life occurrences. Applying the Galtung paradigms yields the following summaries which look for reasons behind the 'obvious' direct violence:

- *Direct* – a young man is shot dead in an urban environment. *Structural* – the neighbourhood lacks effective social services, has poor educational facilities and high unemployment. *Cultural* – the whole area, indeed the whole country, is awash with handguns, a consequence of a pioneering history, and of a fiercely protected written constitution, parts of which are open to misinterpretation, or are even inappropriate, in the modern era.
- *Direct* – a teenager is stabbed to death outside a school. *Structural* – the background is one of racial tensions,

poor educational opportunities, few job prospects for young people, high levels of drug abuse and dealing, mistrust of the police and a well-developed gang culture which uses knives. *Cultural* – the almost universal public and police perception is that this sort of thing is more likely to happen when black youths are involved.

It is striking that, whereas initial analysis proceeds from the top downwards (direct/structural/cultural), effective and permanent solutions to violence-related problems really require the whole approach to be turned upside down. If the cultural and structural aspects can be identified and dealt with, the direct violence they cause will diminish, even fade away. The bleak reality, unfortunately, is that the resources, probably lots of them, needed to make this approach work simply are not there. Either society does not make the connections between direct violence and its underlying social causes; or it accepts the causative links but doesn't care; or it decides that doing anything about it is going to be too expensive. Ironically, however, it will not be as expensive as the cost of dealing with the resultant direct violence, which therefore continues to erupt above the surface from unresolved cultural and structural issues. Resource constraints usually mean that it can then only, and barely, be coped with by a 'fire brigade' approach, attempting to dowse the violence after it erupts.

Spiritual Optometry

Some parts of Christendom's legacy, such as the Church's lapse into sustained violence, have been overt. Others, however, have been more subtle and almost subliminal: here is one example. Early generations of Christians, over many centuries, were mostly illiterate and anyway had no direct access to scripture. As a result, their perceptions of the person of Jesus depended on the only 'lens system' through which they were permitted to see him – that of the Church's teaching and iconography (see pp 33–34). The images they became familiar with were either of a somewhat remote, haloed figure, often lifted up, with celestial robes and benedictive gestures; or related to the gruesome death of a lonely, almost naked figure on a cross or in a grave. We still have such depictions of Jesus with us today in surviving mediaeval art, and of course they are valid, meaningful and often beautiful; but they are only a small part of the picture – literally. They owe much more to stained glass than to Bible study, and bear little resemblance to the down-to-earth and *living* Jesus of the Gospels. To a remarkable extent these misrepresentations, duly updated artistically over the years, have persisted and continue to have almost universal influence. The result is a 'spiritual astigmatism' (distortion) affecting most people's perception of the appearance, behaviour and personality of Jesus. There have also been big 'scotomata' (blind spots) in the Church's central vision, which have blotted out Jesus' teaching about nonviolence, and have also obscured his sheer humanity. A clearer view of the real Jesus in the Gospels only emerged, for those prepared to look and think for themselves, once the Scriptures became available in the vernacular, and when individuals began to shake off the 'think as you are told' restraints of Christendom. (The Anabaptist movement, incidentally, has encouraged Bible study from its beginnings in the 16th century.) *Spiritually speaking, why wear glasses when you can see so very much better without them?!* Be warned, however: Christians discover that undistorted spiritual vision can have challenging consequences, because it makes clear the uncompromising demands Jesus makes of us.

Dissonance and Disavowal

I have argued that the gap between Jesus' teaching and example about violence and nonviolence on the one hand, and mainstream Christian attitudes and practice on the other, is so wide that it can probably only be explained in terms of a spiritual (and cognitive?) dissonance (see pp 67–68), which was insinuated into the gospel by Constantine and his successors and followed up with centuries of dismally effective brainwashing by the Christendom system. The result has been the 'church militant [and military] here in Earth'.

The Church today therefore seems to have a big, longstanding problem; and its apparent unawareness of this fact is, I suggest, a further big problem. The ministry of reconciliation which Christians had been given (2 Cor 5.18–20), and which today's world so desperately needs (32), surely cannot meaningfully begin until two things happen. First, the Church needs to acknowledge and disown its history of violence which runs counter to its founder's most basic teaching. Second, default Christian compliance in the use of violence by nation states today must come to an end. How can these aims be achieved? Probably with the greatest difficulty, at least without the sort of revolution in Christian thinking outlined in Chapter 8 (outlined in 'A Nonviolent Revolution', pp 120–130), because the changes in beliefs and behaviour which would/will be needed are radical. They would require the churches, individually and collectively, to be able to make *and follow through* some such declaration as the following:

- 'We face up to Church violence, and acknowledge its historicity. It happened. Denying or ignoring it are not options.

- We therefore *DISAVOW* it, all of it. We want no part of its heritage or present-day ramifications.

- For the future, we assert that the Church must, and will, stop its acquiescence in any forms of state violence. In addition, it must, and will, formulate *and abide by* Jesus-centred policies covering issues such as the arms trade; overseas military interventions; possession of nuclear, chemical and biological weapons; recruitment of juveniles into the armed forces; and problems arising from Christians serving in the military.'

I would love to be proved wrong, but it seems unlikely, to put it mildly, that anything like the root-and-branch reset implicit in these words will actually happen. That's dispiriting. There is a deep gulf of misunderstanding between Jesus' teaching and example on the one hand, and the Christendom legacy of 'Onward, Christian soldiers' on the other; and at present there seem to be only two bridges across this chasm. One bridge, called 'just war theory', is likely to collapse if any weight at all is put on it (see pp 77–82). The other bridge, called 'dissonance' (see pp 67-68), has some traffic of thoughtful but confused-looking people scurrying to and fro, trying to make sense of their disparate experiences on either side of the divide. Many Christians, however, appear to have little awareness of the gap, and no interest in attempting to cross it. For them, sadly, the chasm remains.

Moving On

The first part of this book tried to summarise the violence perpetrated by or on behalf of the Church, often specifically in the name of Christ, over at least 12 centuries. It was behaviour which arose from Christendom's almost perverse disregard of some basic elements of the teaching and example of Jesus. It has caused so much hatred, so much destruction, so much contempt for human life, that *sometimes* we might *almost* feel like joining the 18th-century men of enlightenment to ask, 'Where could God possibly be in all of this?' Only sometimes and only almost; because, unlike them, we have an immediate answer. We point straight to Jesus. *That* is where God is

- Jesus on a hillside teaching about his Kingdom (Mat 5.1–7:27);
- Jesus demonstrating who my neighbour is and what I should do about it (Luke 10.25–27);
- Jesus *taking up his cross, with all its consequences of suffering and death, and calling on us, his disciples, to do likewise* (Luke 9.23);

- Jesus going to his death on our behalf, as nonviolently as a sacrificial lamb (Isa 53.7);
- the risen Jesus demonstrating, during a picnic breakfast on a seashore, how forgiveness and reconciliation work in practice (John 21.15–19).

THIS is where God was and is. Jesus is in all human life and experience.

THIS is what we believe.

THIS is the Gospel. It's the Gospel which took the Roman Empire by storm, and which the Church should have been proclaiming, in active nonviolent love, to all nations for the last 1600 years.

'I am the Light of the World' (John 8.12)

'This little light of mine, I'm gonna let it shine.'
There's a lot of darkness in the Church's history. Of course, not all of it is down to violence. As an antidote to the gloom, whatever its causes, and also to anticipate more positive and affirmative things to come in the final two chapters, what follows is a brief celebration of light. Because there's always been lots of that too.

Even in the darkest times – think, for example, of ordinary folk during the Thirty Years' War (see p 45) – individual flickers of the Light of Christ have coalesced into brighter beams which have pierced the shadows of ignorant and violent religion. God uses true disciples as mirrors to reflect his light into the darkest places. 'You are the light of the world' (Matt 5.14); this refers to those who serve their neighbours in love, and try to love their enemies, thereby transforming both their own lives and those of others (Matt 5.16). They have their rewards; God bless them all.

A constant and especially bright beacon through the centuries has been the Church's continuous record of care of the sick, the helpless and the outcast. As the Early Church blossomed, pagan neighbours were astonished to see the care given by Christians to the most vulnerable, in not only their own but also in neighbouring non-Christian communities. This was day-to-day *agape* in action. Furthermore, when two pandemics swept through the Empire, in 16–-180 AD and again in 249–262, both with devastating consequences, the light of Christ shone with comforting brightness in the terrified pagan darkness. Those who could escape the cities fled to the countryside, but it was Christians who tended to remain behind, ministering to the sick and dying living in ramshackle city tenements, regardless of whether they were Christian or pagan (4). As Stark has commented, against a backdrop of appalling hygiene and non-existent sanitation, even the most basic nursing care would have had a big impact on survival rates.

And it still does, 18 centuries on. As just one of many possible examples, there have been moving reports of the activities of Christian charities working in the sprawling slums of Delhi in India as the Covid pandemic wreaked dreadful havoc there (May 2021). One such is Asha, whose volunteers brought basic health care to those struck down by the disease. It was noticeable, and noticed, that where they worked, mortality was reduced.

They were, of course, far from the only people bringing the practical, merciful light of Christ to those in mortal need during the pandemic. Workers in our UK NHS gave this same devoted care, day and night. Some were Christians. The others? – 'Truly I tell you, just as you did it to one of the least of these … you did it to me' (Matt 25.40).

During the present Covid pandemic in the UK, particularly in the early stages when there was fear of the unknown, it became apparent that the most vulnerable families were being stricken by their precarious economic situations as well as by the virus. It was often church communities, even individual clergy (at least two of whom, in different towns, were featured on the national TV news), who worked tirelessly to make a difference in the name of Jesus, and to offer practical support to those in most need.

The Emperor Julian attempted but failed to revive paganism during his brief reign in 361–363. Among other challenges he was unable to meet, he recognised that a pagan welfare system comparable to that in Christian communities would be needed, but would probably be unachievable. He is said to have commented, 'These impious Galileans not only feed their own poor, but ours also: welcoming them into their *agapai*, they attract them, as children are attracted, with cakes' (37). They still do.

Bright Lights

With a little thought, we can all compile our personal roll calls of those we revere most as beacons of nonviolent light through the ages. Their contributions have embraced everything from changing individual lives to altering the course of history. My own list would include Brother Lawrence (38), George Fox, William Penn, John Woolman (39*), Dorothy Day, Nelson Mandela (40*), Desmond Tutu, Mahatma Gandhi (40*), Corrie ten Boom and Martin Luther King Jr. (For special mention of

Dietrich Bonhoeffer, see (41*)). That's far from exhaustive, and one could add many more. Indeed, the making of lists is probably invidious in that so many more people, whether known or unknown to us individually, deserve recognition.

Our Celtic Christian forbears identified 'thin places', where Heaven and Earth become very close, and any barrier between the two may disappear briefly. This is probably a very ancient insight. In recent times, such thin places seem to be in locations and at times when the Holy Spirit is intensely active. Many of us will have taken part in 'thin' worship. Thin places which come immediately to mind are the Lee Abbey movement in Devon, London and elsewhere; Scargill in Yorkshire; the Iona community in Scotland and Taizé in France. There must be dozens more, together with time-and-place bursts of light around annual gatherings like New Wine, Spring Harvest and the Keswick Convention. We could extend this idea to include 'thin times', which would 'explain' revivals and phenomena like the Toronto Blessing. With a commitment to nonviolence at these times/places, Heaven would find it easier still to break through.

Occasionally (is it really that infrequent?), the veil between Heaven and Earth really does disappear. There are examples in the Bible. In the Old Testament, Elisha's servant, scared witless by a seemingly impossible military situation, found himself surrounded by a host of heavenly beings reassuringly on *his* side (2 Kings 6.17). Many years later, heralding 'peace on earth', a hillside near Bethlehem was visited by 'a multitude of the heavenly host', and bathed in the brilliant light of the glory of God, and in glorious singing (Luke 2. 9–14). To bring this idea into the near present, some years ago my wife and I were at Lee Abbey, where among the guests was a boy (with Down syndrome) in his early teens, clearly with a vivid and lively spirituality all of his own. During one session, when there had been beautiful singing and a real sense of God's close presence with us, this young man seemed preoccupied with the ceiling of the tall room in which we were gathered. Later, we asked him what had caught his attention. 'Oh', he said, matter-of-factly, 'I was watching the angels'.

There are three denominations within the worldwide Church – the Religious Society of Friends (Quakers), the Church of the Brethren and the Mennonites/Anabaptists – which are known as the Historic Peace Churches because active pursuit of peace and nonviolent opposition to all aspects of war have been central to their beliefs and witness since their foundation. It is no surprise that three of the names on my personal shortlist of bright lights (see above) were members of the Society of Friends; several of the truly Christ-like people I personally have met have been Quakers.

In the UK, there are several hundred organisations specifically set up to work for peace in various ways and contexts. Of these, 22 specifically Christian agencies cooperate in the Network of Christian Peace Organisations (NCPO) (which, incidentally, gives some idea of the extent to which Christians working for peace are outnumbered, see p 51). Some have set themselves national and some international remits; most are small; all are committed to work for peace as a specifically Christian obligation. Typical of these is the Christian International Peace Service (CHIPS), which does below-the-radar work to promote reconciliation and peace in war- and violence-torn parts of the UK and in the wider world.

Finally, we can draw comfort and inspiration from the constant stream of individual acts of forgiveness and reconciliation, large and small, which are taking place all the time. Some are so extraordinary that they flash across the news media like shooting stars, and cause widespread astonishment. These 'meteors' have included stories which emerged from the work of the Truth and Reconciliation Commission in South Africa; the response of the Amish community – to forgive, and to rally round and support the family of the *perpetrator* – when a gunman shot dead children and adults in one of their schools in 2006; and the mother in Liverpool whose 12-year-old son had been murdered, by a gang whom she publicly forgave and privately worked to understand in order to help and support them.

For it is the God who said, 'Let light shine out of darkness,' who has shone in our hearts to give the light of the knowledge of the glory of God in the face of Jesus Christ. (2 Cor 4.6)

Active Christian Nonviolence

In the previous chapters we put violence in its place, and then indulged briefly in some spiritual sunbathing. That's all very well, but what are we going to *do* about it? What difference is commitment to non-violence going to make, both in our own lives and also collectively among God's people? How can nonviolence become more than a helpful attitude of mind? How do we make it part of our Christian discipleship? What is Active Christian Nonviolence (30)(42) anyway? We can begin, at least, to answer these important questions in this chapter.

Straight away, there are several things Active Christian Nonviolence certainly *is*:

- it is what Jesus taught and modelled for us in his own behaviour, suffering and death;
- it is a spiritual discipline in our lives, strengthening our faith in the risen Lord Jesus;
- it is something *active*, with which we withstand evil, in ourselves and in the world;
- it is a means by which we can acquire a special attitude of mind, clarified by Paul (Phil 2. 5–8) – '*Let this mind*

be in you that was in Christ Jesus who, though he was in the form of God, did not regard equality with God as something to be exploited, but emptied himself … and became obedient to the point of death – even death on a cross' (italics are, of course, mine).

Then there are several things it equally certainly is *not*:

- it is not passive;
- it does not look away, or run away, or do doormat stuff;
- it is not easy, and is sometimes, perhaps even often, difficult and/or costly;
- it is not necessarily safe.

The last point needs further brief comment. In the UK at present, there is little likelihood that nonviolent activity will lead directly to injury or death. However, in an uncertain future (see a Nonviolent Revolution?, pp 120–130) and an increasingly secular society, that could change. A look at the USA, where the country being awash with guns certainly doesn't help, shows how standing up for what is right can, and occasionally does, lead to loss of life or to injury. We need to be prepared to suffer, and even to die, for what we believe – **that is the Way of the Cross.**

It's very important to be clear about one thing – it's not necessary to be a Christian in order to believe in and practise nonviolence. There are many conscientious, caring people working for peace and towards an absence of violence, who do so either with the motivation of a non-Christian faith, or with humanist and humane incentives which have nothing to do with religious belief. Some are full-time, professional peacemakers. Many more – millions actually, in certain circumstances (see below) – are ordinary folk who are prepared to stand up if necessary, in nonviolent and peaceful protest. In these activities, even the focussed ones, Christians dedicated to peace are heavily outnumbered. Given how many Christians there are supposed to be in the world, and given also the fundamentally nonviolent message of the Gospel (which Mahatma Gandhi, for one, recognised), that is a deeply shaming situation. Nevertheless, we work with our non-Christian nonviolent friends towards common goals, of course we do. So what's the difference?

The difference is motivation – why we do as we do. It's not just to make the world a better place – although we believe it will do that. It's not just in the cause of justice, especially for the downtrodden – although we hope to contribute to that as well. It's not even to get a warm glow that We're Doing the Right Thing – although that may happen from time to time as a welcome side effect. We do as we do because *Jesus told us to* – to love our enemies, just as he did and does, as a manifestation of his love for us and for them. He took anger and violence and hate – ours and theirs – with him to death on the cross. God's love is unconditional; so should ours be. We do what we do in his strength, not ours. Which is simple (that is to say, not complicated), often difficult (that is to say, not easy), and always worth striving for. Again, *that is the Way of the Cross*.

Spiritual Discipline

Does spiritual discipline sound unfamiliar and a bit of a turn-off? It needn't. It doesn't mean sackcloth and ashes. It doesn't necessarily involve fasting, although some people find a degree of abstinence at times very helpful. It must involve prayer, loads of it, both personal and communal. We are also required to 'let go and let God'. In his helpful book, *Who Are Our Enemies and How Do We Love Them?* (29), Hyung Jin Kim Sun writes, 'It takes courage and risk to give up our sense of control and to trust in God's way. For this reason, love towards enemies and nonviolent engagement embody spiritual discipline … Learning to trust God is a lifelong journey that requires intentional effort and a long period of discipline … Seeking to discipline our sense of control is a profoundly spiritual endeavour.'

So, in the style of the rather silly jokes which were once in vogue (e.g. what do you get when you cross a sheep with a kangaroo? Answer – a woolly jumper), what do you get when you cross spiritual discipline with active nonviolence? Answer – *a spirituality of active nonviolence*. This term, coined by David Augsburger, is explained in his book *Dissident Discipleship* (41), and I cannot do better than to quote his own summary.

'A spirituality of active nonviolence –
- chooses faithfulness to the way of Jesus, the way of the cross, over personal security; chooses the practice of nonviolent love over defensive, reactive rage; rejects resorting, even regretfully or remorsefully, to violent self-defence as less than the spirituality of the cross.
- refuses to join the spiral of violence-retaliation-violence-revenge-violence-recrimination-violence-retribution.

- seeks a constructive process for addressing, resolving, and reconciling conflicts, and seeks to transform the system that engendered the conflict in the first place.
- is an act of faith in the nonviolent God revealed to us in the non-resistant Jesus, who confronted evil with all his power but without abuse of power.
- seeks the truth, the opponent's truth as well as its own; seeks genuine human social concern, believing that humans are meant to love and be loved.
- is a politics of repentance and reconciliation that works for transformation of broken systems, for healing of wounded persons, for change in the human order.
- is not optimistic about human conflict – it takes evil very seriously – but believes in the reality of good even more than the reality of evil.'

There you have it, succinct, comprehensive and challenging. Further comment would be superfluous, except perhaps to suggest that to 'read, mark, learn and inwardly digest' (43*) that summary would be time extremely well spent.

The Way of the Cross

I have explained my use of this phrase (see p 18). However it's a recurring theme in this book, particularly in this chapter, and is so important that it needs further brief comment:

- The Way of the Cross is an ongoing experience, not a theological concept.
- It requires the sort of discipline we've just been talking about.

- It's a full-time commitment. Jesus said, 'If any want to become my followers, let them deny themselves [discipline again] and take up their cross *daily* and follow me' (Luke 9.23, emphasis mine). Would-be part-timers need not apply.

- It can be very hard. Life's like that. We don't know why, and we aren't told why. But –

- Jesus walks the Way of the Cross with us, with each of us individually, and as closely as we will let him. He's been there already, more than we can ever know. He understands our own frailties much better than we do. Even if/when he does not seem that close because of our lapses (as somebody observed, 'when God seems far away, who has moved?'), he *is* there, always. The presence of Jesus on each and every individual's Way of the Cross is one of our faith's greatest blessings. (Mat 28.20; Heb 13.5–6).

Jesus' Third Way

Jesus' teaching about how to respond to a confrontation with violence is often construed as impractical idealism. 'Turn the other cheek' has acquired a doormat aura. 'Going the second mile' has come to imply super-acquiescence. And in particular, 'Do not resist an evildoer' appears to suggest passive submission to any form of violence; which, if true, would-be dismal advice for battered wives, victims of bullies and others who are on the receiving end of gratuitous violence.

Of course, Jesus didn't mean any of that. But what did he

mean? Walter Wink (28) helps us, yet again, this time with an intriguing exegesis of Matthew 5.38–41. Wink suggested that Jesus, teaching a crowd of ordinary 1st-century Palestinian folk, was giving examples of a third way, something which is neither submission nor aggression. His listeners would have had no problems with his illustrations, taken, as so often in his teaching, from their everyday lives. We should try to hear and understand Jesus' words from that same perspective if we can.

Here is the relevant passage:

'You have heard that it was said, "An eye for an eye and a tooth for a tooth". But I say to you, do not resist an evildoer. But if anyone strikes you on the right cheek, turn the other also; and if anyone wants to sue you and take your coat, give your cloak as well; and if anyone forces you to go one mile, go also the second mile' (Mat 5.38–41)

Let's look in turn at those four 'I say to you' sentences.

- 'Do not resist an evildoer'. Something usually gets lost in translation here. Matthew's gospel has come down to us in Greek, in which the word in v 39 which is rendered 'resist' is *antistenai*, which literally means to stand (*stenai*) against (*anti*). The same word was used in the Septuagint, the Greek translation of the Old Testament, widely used in Jesus' day, in the military context of two armies going out, meeting each other, and standing almost breastplate to breastplate before starting to fight. A 21st-century equivalent might be two professional boxers at a pre-fight weigh-in, full of adrenalin and testosterone, eyeballing each other. Of course, the Christian who is faced with that kind of posturing and intent shouldn't reply in kind; Jesus didn't need to spell that out. But neither did he mean 'just roll over and give in regardless', an interpretation which is often suggested, but which the context and the words used simply do not support. Instead, he was saying, in the context of a stand-off, 'do not respond to evil in an aggressive manner'; or 'don't react violently against the one who is evil.' We should take that advice, and carry it over to the rest of Jesus' teaching in this passage.

- '… if anyone strikes you on the right cheek, turn the other also'. It helps to walk this through with another person. The first point to remember is that the 1st-century left hand, reserved for sanitary purposes such as bum-wiping, would not have been involved in any delivery or exchange of blows. The only way to strike someone on the *right* cheek with the right hand is with the *back* of the hand. Go on, try it. A backhander was the blow used to put someone in their place, a sharp reminder of their inferior status: masters backhanded slaves; husbands, wives; parents, children; Romans, Jews. Now, Jesus said, if that happens to you, turn the other cheek. It then becomes impossible for the aggressor to repeat the back-handed blow – on the right cheek because the victim's nose is in the way; or on the left cheek because it's impossible to hit the left cheek with the *back* of the right hand. Again, go on, try it. The only remaining option would be to strike the other person on the left cheek, or on the nose turned to the right, *with either the palm of the open right hand (a slap) or with the right fist.* Such blows would be understood to be between people of equal social status, not a back-handed put-down. Note carefully that Jesus is not advocating the use of any violence whatsoever: there is nothing aggressive about turning the other cheek. What is clear is that the aggressor's attempt to demean the recipient with a backhander will not work, and that any future exchanges, as between people of equal status and worth, will be nonviolent. Note carefully also, that this has nothing whatsoever to do with submission or door-matting. This is neither fight nor flight; it's a *third way*.

- '… if anyone wants to sue you and take your coat, give your cloak as well'. Land ownership had special resonance for Jews because it meant personal shares of the Chosen Land, given by God as part of his covenant deal with his chosen people. By the 1st century, however, indebtedness involving land had become rife, mainly because of harsh Roman imperial taxation which had a strong trickle-down effect. Rates of interest were financially crippling, and peasants such as those listening to Jesus had often had their land prised from them to pay taxation debts. Several of Jesus' parables feature debtors apparently struggling to cope. The poorest, who owned nothing but the clothes they stood up in, could nevertheless still be taken to court by rapacious creditors who were allowed by law to demand one of the two items of clothing the debtor would be wearing, tunic or cloak but not both, as collateral. Jesus' suggestion was that they should indeed hand over *both* tunic (coat) *and* cloak, leaving them naked in court. Nakedness was a powerful taboo for Jews; and to reduce someone to that state, especially in a semi-public place such as a courtroom, would reflect very badly on the person responsible for the humiliation, rather than on the poor victim, who had almost nothing to lose anyway. The attempt to exploit the defenceless would therefore have backfired on the aggressor. Note that once again no violence is being advocated. Another way, a *third way* between aggression and abjection, is possible.

- '… if anyone forces you to go one mile, go also the second mile'. Once again, Jesus' hearers would have known at once what he was talking about. For several centuries, Palestine – indeed the whole 'corridor' down the Eastern edge of the Mediterranean – had been under foreign occupation, by the Persians followed by the Syrians, and finally in the 1st century by the Romans. Soldiers were everywhere to subjugate the locals. Any male civilian was required by law to assist a Roman soldier on demand, by carrying his equipment for him for a distance of one mile. The limit was enforced to prevent civilian unrest or insurrection on the grounds of over-exploitation. It followed that a carry of over a mile would have had the soldier in breach of regulations, and liable to being disciplined or punished according to the circumstances. Jesus' suggestion would therefore put the soldier on the defensive without the use of any force. This would be another moral victory over the Powers of Domination (see pp 30–31) without the use of any violence, and another example of a *third way.*

These are homely yet powerful illustrations of a different approach, neither fleeing nor fighting but quietly making a nonviolent point, often defusing the situation and never aggravating it. It's often an effective means of countering violence, and people can be trained in the necessary skills, to enhance any nonviolent protests they make. The two great 20th-century exponents of nonviolence, Mahatma Gandhi and Martin Luther King Jr, would certainly have endorsed it. Wink wrote a separate small book about Jesus' Third Way (which may no longer be available – I'm still searching). As the end of apartheid approached in South Africa and widespread violence was anticipated, he smuggled both himself and the book into the country (from which he had been banned), to help train clergy and others in nonviolent resistance. In the event bloodshed was less, and less protracted, than many had feared. To what extent did awareness of Jesus' Third Way contribute to that outcome, I wonder?

The Effectiveness of Active Nonviolence

Which leads neatly into a discussion of whether nonviolence can work. It may surprise many people to know that the short answer is definitely *YES*, in many circumstances. It is not difficult to justify that statement.

Consider these well-known events from a nonviolence perspective:

- India gained its independence from British colonial rule in 1950, with relatively little violence and bloodshed. This was the culmination of campaigns of nonviolence and civil disobedience organised and led by Mahatma Gandhi over many years. (My remarks obviously do not cover Partition, which occurred shortly afterwards and was, tragically, a bloodbath.)

- Martin Luther King Jr led an explicitly nonviolent campaign for civil rights in America between 1955 and his assassination in 1968. Its achievements are remarkable, and the ongoing movement, still nonviolent in a country where prejudice is deep-seated and guns are everywhere, might be said to be a work in progress.

- As already indicated above, following decades of politically motivated violence, and several years of secret negotiations with Nelson Mandela while he was still in prison, Mandela was released in 1990 and apartheid came to an end in 1993. There was, sadly, some violence but on nothing like the scale which had been widely feared.

- Following the fall of the Berlin Wall in 1989, and the subsequent collapse of the Soviet Union, millions of citizens in countries across Eastern Europe demonstrated peacefully and successfully for political change and the establishment of democracies. Only in one country were troops involved and shots fired.

- During WW2, Lithuania was first occupied by the Soviet Union, then by Germany, then once more by Soviet Russia in 1944. Expecting Western help which never came, Lithuanians fought an unsuccessful and costly guerrilla war until 1952, when there was a deliberate switch *by the government* to a policy of nonviolent resistance. Many lives were saved thereby, and independence was eventually re-established in 1990, a whole year before the formal dissolution of the Soviet Union.

Social and political sciences are increasingly recognising that nonviolence can be a force for good to be reckoned with. Hyung Jin Kim Sun (29) references published studies from Harvard University, examining more than 300 nonviolent and violent campaigns around the world between 1990 and 2006. To the researchers' surprise, nonviolent resistance movements proved to be twice as likely to achieve full or partial success as violent ones. One reason, rather obviously once one thinks of it, seemed to be that nonviolence allows, indeed encourages, mass participation which, by definition, includes a much wider range of people than those who would be directly involved in armed struggle. Research showed that the larger the number of people directly involved in protest, the greater the chance of a successful outcome. Around 3.5 per cent of the population was found to be a threshold above which nonviolent success was virtually assured, but much smaller numbers could also be effective. These reputable findings are remarkable and immensely encouraging.

Very sadly, of course, fallen human nature being what it is, nonviolence often doesn't seem to work. The protests in Hong Kong in 2019–20, and in Myanmar in 2021, both started peacefully, but were met with such a ferocious and implacable reaction from the Powers that nonviolence was swamped and, when both sides started fighting, the outcomes were inevitable. Particularly high levels of outrage about perceived injustices on the protest side met Powers with an unusually low reactive threshold on the other. The result was violence from both sides, with such inequality of fire power that resistance was crushed. We have to conclude that the Domination System still has an iron grip in many circumstances.

Some 'what-iffery' is probably unavoidable, and Hitler is usually held up as the example of a potential threat where nonviolence would not have worked, and the use of force was therefore inevitable. That isn't necessarily true. Organised nonviolent responses to Nazism were sadly few and small scale, but *those which were tried were successful.*

- With a lead from the Orthodox Church, Bulgarians resisted all collaboration with Nazi decrees related to the round-up and deportation of Jews. They marched in mass demonstrations, and swamped the authorities with written protests, to the point of systems paralysis. As a direct result, the Nazis gave up trying, and all Bulgaria's Jewish citizens were saved.

- There was similar nonviolent resistance in Finland which saved all but six of Finland's Jews.
- In Denmark, with the involvement of almost everybody, Jews were either smuggled into (neutral) Sweden or successfully hidden.
- Similar actions with similar results occurred in Norway, where passive resistance also interfered with the setting up of a puppet Nazi collaborative government.
- In Italy many Jews were saved by official and civilian nonviolent obstructive tactics.

There's no reason to assume that widespread, well-organised nonviolence would inevitably have been crushed by the Nazis. Lives would certainly have been lost, but probably *far* fewer than the casualties caused by the use of force by all sides in WW2. Unfortunately, widespread organised resistance was not forthcoming. The myth of redemptive violence took over, and the rest is, as they say, horrible history.

There is a special irony in the circumstances surrounding the collapse of tyranny in Eastern Europe in the early 1990s (27). Following Augustine's (NOT Jesus') lead, theologians have been earnestly persuading Christians for 16 centuries that the gospel supports the use of violence. It took a peaceful outpouring of literally millions of citizens onto the streets of one officially *atheist* country after another to demonstrate how effective Jesus' teaching about nonviolence can be as a means of liberation – whether the liberators are aware of it or not.

I want finally to reiterate and emphasise the very important point I made earlier in this chapter, about outcomes. For those of us who pursue unconditional nonviolence as part of Christian discipleship, we go down the nonviolent path because Jesus did so first, and he calls us to do the same. Whatever positive results are nonviolently attained, although they are obviously important, they are secondary. We try to be obedient, and we commit outcomes to him. That is not a logical approach, it is a spiritual one. ***It is the Way of the Cross.***

A Nonviolent Revolution?

One of my hopes for this book is that it might contribute, in a small way, to the start of a revolution. Yes, really. Because something of the sort will be needed to shake Christian thinking about violence out of its centuries-old ruts of complacency and self-deception.

All of us who are disciples of Jesus, the Prince of Peace, are should-be revolutionaries, and we should be issuing challenges such as this one:

> We are called to unite as those who seek the Way of the Cross; as those who follow Jesus' example wherever that takes us; and as those who witness in our daily lives to the redemptive power of *non*violence. By so doing, **we transform ALL our relationships** – with God, with our fellow human beings, with ourselves, and with creation. That in turn makes reconciliation, of all kinds and at all levels, not only possible but inevitable.

Please just pause to take in the implications of what you have just read – and then read it again. Think about it. It is indeed revolutionary, and I believe it to be true.

A positive response to that challenge by any person both transforms the life of that individual and also greatly increases the effectiveness of the fellowship of which he/she is a member. A movement of this kind among God's people on earth would, among its other consequences, create a distinctive way ahead for parts of the Church wishing to commit to uncompromising nonviolence. What might such developments look like? The question is timely because substantial and probably irreversible changes in the structures and organisation of the Church are likely in any case, as we shall see. There will be opportunities to be seized which could amount to something like an ecclesiastical metamorphosis, a transformation of practical Christianity.

Collectively, those of us within the Protestant Churches today for whom 'evangelism' and 'revival' are familiar buzzwords, like to point to increasing numbers attending lively churches, successful church plants, more and more Alpha courses – advertised on the sides of buses, forsooth – and news of thriving churches in far-away places. For some time past, the message seems to have been, 'One final push and, with the help of the Holy Spirit, some sort of golden age, possibly even God's kingdom here on earth, will dawn'. Will it? In the UK at least, a look at both rural and urban ministry in most denominations, and a quick horrified glance at the surrounding strife- and poverty-torn world in the throes of climate change, suggests that it won't, at least not imminently; and that, if it does, it won't look like anything we might have imagined. Objective appraisals suggest that most Christians will have to adjust to working in and for churches which are shrinking in terms of societal influence, and are hemmed in spiritually by resurgent paganism.

Post-Christendom

Stuart Murray's book *Post-Christendom* (7), has the subtitle *Church and mission in a strange new world*. It outlines a growing school of thought which sees the apparently terminal decline of Christendom today as a tipping point in the history of the worldwide Church. It gives a succinct account of Christendom's history, and proposes that the church–state relationships on which Western civilisation is said to have been built – and on which formalities such as church attendance, weddings, christenings and funerals have depended – have been under siege, especially since the 1960s, and are now crumbling irretrievably. We are now, it is being suggested, in a post-Christendom era.

It is certainly true that the numbers of people attending church in Europe, the USA and Canada have been dropping, and there's a general disinterest in what are supposed to be uniquely Christian beliefs, attitudes and practices. Increasingly, the Church is perceived by those outside it to be irrelevant to society's needs, and unable to address the pressing issues of today's world. It's also likely that the UK 2021 National Census (results to be published in 2022) will show – for the first time since decennial censuses were introduced 220 years ago – that a *minority* of people in this country now identify themselves as 'Christian'. (It is, of course, far from clear what most people actually mean by that.)

Globally, the situation varies for historical reasons. From the 4th century, the Christendom complex took over and defined what Church became in Western Europe. However, those countries which were mainly 'Christianised' by outreach from Europe during the colonial era (principally the 19th century) absorbed Christendom ideals and practices into their cultures to widely varying extents. They may therefore react to its demise in different ways. In response to rapidly falling numbers of even nominal Christians in Europe (also in Canada, Australia and New Zealand), there is also a reverse missionary movement under way from churches in Africa and Asia, to re-evangelise an increasingly unchurched and pagan West.

Furthermore, while the general movement in numbers, which are, or course, not the whole picture, is downwards, sometimes steeply so, there are places and situations which buck this trend. As suggested above, charismatic churches and some church-planting initiatives in the UK report increasing numbers attending; and, perhaps rather surprisingly, cathedrals and abbey churches here are thriving as centres of worship. In South America, Africa and parts of Asia, protestant evangelical and charismatic churches are booming.

Murray suggests (7) that we are entering a period of 'adjustment', which is likely to last perhaps 40 or so years, during which time the worn-out old will be replaced by the as-yet-uncertain new. There will be opportunities for positive and radical change, in a spiritual and social climate which has yet to take shape. Watch this space.

As control moves from historical Christendom to new and unfamiliar structures and activities – that is to say, from a complacent status quo to something much more uncertain and challenging – big changes will be inevitable. Murray has summarised some of these, which he describes as a series of *transitions*:

- *from the centre to the margins.* The Christian story and churches will no longer be central in community life.
- *from majority to minority.* Christians will be outnumbered.
- *from settled to sojourners.* Christians will become resident aliens ((17) – see below).
- *from privilege to plurality.* Christians will become one community among many in a plural society.
- *from control to witness.* Influence will be exercised by Christian witness, not by historical privilege.
- *from maintenance to mission.* There will no longer be an emphasis on maintaining the historical status quo, but on mission in a contested and competitive environment.
- *from institution to movement.* Churches will no longer be representing an institution; they must become an active Christian movement.

In part depending how quickly changes occur, that looks like a series of recipes for uncertainty and controversy, at least in the short term. What will the outcomes and reactions be?

Some people, including key players in whatever happens, will welcome change. Others will probably resent and resist it. There will be opportunities. There will be losses. These are indeed challenging times!

Resident Aliens

Hauerwas' and Willimon's book (17) has this title and offers an American perspective which in large part also has universal relevance. Like Murray, the authors also identify the 1960s as a watershed. They are robustly critical of the apologetic, defensive theologies formulated by the academic Church during the past 150 years in response to science and 'reason'. They see the marginalisation of churches as a challenge and, above all, an opportunity. They argue persuasively that the task of the Church is not to explain or justify Christianity to the world, but to live the Gospel in such a way that it becomes irresistibly attractive, so that people will want to come along for the lifelong ride. And only Christ, they insist, has the right answers for those with questions about the meaning of life and the human condition.

These authors also hope that marginalised churches will become 'free to embrace our roots, to resemble more closely the synagogue – that is to say, a faith community that does not ask the world to do what it can only do for itself.' Yes, absolutely, in terms of independence from vestiges of Christendom control, and as resident aliens in a pagan wider world. However, one key characteristic of orthodox Jewish community life is bypassed, or at least not mentioned, in that suggestion; namely its manifestly inward-looking stance, which is the exact opposite of how future church communities must orientate themselves if they are to attract those around them. Indeed, one of the biggest challenges for the post-Christendom Church will be how to reach out to the world without compromising its own integrity. *It can be done!* The thriving Early Church must have been brilliantly successful at doing exactly that. How? I suggest that it was, firstly, *explicitly a nonviolent church* (see pp 24–30). Secondly, the *agape* (see pp 68–69) referred to by the disgruntled pagan Emperor Julian must have been one of the Early Church's most appealing characteristics. The combination of nonviolence and *agape* was evidently irresistible, and it can be that again.

What's in a Name?

A growing commitment to active nonviolence has the potential to become a new movement transcending denominational boundaries. It would identify and unite members within established denominations who want to commit to something new, different and potentially inclusive, and for whom the Way of the Cross comes to symbolise, among other things, an affirmation of nonviolence. The challenge on (see p 120), or something similar, could provide a focal point, and the Spirituality of Active Nonviolence, outlined in the previous chapter (see pp 107–108) (42), is a good summary of the commitment and discipline which would be involved. This would be no walk in the spiritual park, no cosy club. To emphasise the point yet again, such discipleship is potentially very costly, even to the point of giving up one's own life because of faith in Jesus, should it ever come to that.

Does such a movement or trend within existing Churches, assuming it comes about, need a distinctive name? The answer partly depends on where things start to happen. In North America, and possibly elsewhere as well, the existing flourishing Anabaptist and similar networks would welcome and nurture anyone wishing to commit to active nonviolence for the first time. I cannot speak for mainland Europe, but for any nonviolence 'converts' in the UK, support is more low profile at present (see pp 17–18). In these circumstances, a name might provide collective support, at least in the short term. (It should be discarded if/ when it becomes a distraction.) My suggestion would be *New Peace Church* (or possibly New Peace Movement), each word underlining something important: a *New* emphasis for many Christians; having *Peace,* that is to say an absence of violence in all its forms, at its heart; and remaining part of the *Church,* the company of all disciples of Jesus here on Earth.

In the short term, most members of a New Peace Church in the UK and Europe would be scattered, a bit like corn seed, across existing Churches and denominations, partly because there is no other obvious place for them to go at present. Elsewhere, in North America (and South America? Africa? Asia?) for example, they would either already be members of existing peace-orientated churches (45*), or would swell their ranks if newly committed to nonviolence. Only God knows what the longer term will hold for us all. I wonder if we are ready for whatever it turns out to be.

Over the past 600 years the Church of England has become so inextricably entangled with the State – socially, politically and even militarily – that a complete separation is probably unachievable. One might also ask whether there would be any point, particularly if the C of E and other denominations of today really are in terminal decline. So far as England is concerned, such a 'disestablishment' would at least represent a definitive reversal of Henry VIII's wilful 16th-century misuse of the Church/State union, which in turn was based on Constantine's disastrous take-over of the Church by the State 1,700 years ago. It would also, in theory at least, finally remove the State from its constitutional place at the heart of the C of E, which is a spiritual nonsense (44*). Does any of this really matter? Will the spiritually alive parts of the C of E survive and thrive? What about untethered Anglicanism in Wales, Scotland, Ireland and elsewhere in the world? What about Non-conformity, Roman Catholicism, Eastern Orthodoxy?

The Kingdom of God (36*)

Reading the inscriptions on UK war memorials from time to time (46*), I have been struck particularly by the concept of allegiance to King and Country (I have commented on this already, see p 40). This has led me to reflect that we Christians are, in general, not nearly aware enough, or 'proud' enough, of our primary allegiance to *our* King – *Jesus*; and to *his* country – the *Kingdom of God*. This must surely, if necessary, come before any loyalty and obligation we have to a secular state. Does it? For which King and Country would and should we be prepared to lay down our lives? Seriously, we need to get our priorities, our citizenship and our sense of patriotism sorted out (36*). During the persecutions in the earliest years of the Church, Christians were required to declare their allegiance either to Jesus and his Kingdom, or to the Roman Emperor and Empire. We may not be forced to choose in that stark binary way, but are we prepared to stand right up for what we believe, regardless of the consequences? *Really* prepared? In the 21st century most of us are relatively unlikely to face life or death choices, even with an uncertain future ahead of the Church; but we are more likely than ever before to have to declare where our primary allegiance lies. For example, in situations where some jobs become closed to committed Christians (not at all far-fetched in a future militantly pagan society), how would we respond? If a particular career path involved accepting compromised ethical standards, would we be prepared to see the situation clearly, to stand up and be counted for what we believe, and why, and to declare where our overriding loyalties lie, regardless of the personal and other consequences?

There are 140 references to the Kingdom of God, or Kingdom of Heaven (47*), in the New Testament, 114 of these in the Gospels. It was what John the Baptist proclaimed (Mat 3.2); it was a major theme of Jesus' ministry (Luke 8.1); it was taught by him using a stream of parables (Mat 13.24–47); and it was misinterpreted by disciples whose idea of a kingdom, perhaps understandably, was earthly power and glory (Mark 10.35–39).

Every time we say the Lord's Prayer, we ask for God's Kingdom to come, and his will to be done, 'on earth as in

Heaven'. We talk about Kingdom work, some of us wondering, if we're honest, what that really means. The Kingdom of God is in time yet outside time; in Heaven (that elusive dimension) and also here on Earth; and already here but not here yet. Those are all enigmatic paradoxes. God's Kingdom has been revealed to us incrementally through Jesus' incarnation, ministry, death, resurrection and ascension; and by the power of the Holy Spirit since Pentecost. The Grand Finale, which will also be the Grand Opening of the New Age – another paradox – is yet to come. We are assured that 'the kingdom of the world [will] become the kingdom of our Lord and of his Messiah, and he will reign for ever and ever' (Rev 11.15). That Kingdom, before and also beyond any of this world, is the one of which we are citizens already: it is *our* 'King and Country'. And that timetable, we should never forget, gives ample ongoing scope in the here and now for the prince of darkness to try to disrupt progress towards the coming of the Kingdom. We cannot afford to relax for a moment from this *spiritual* warfare, until we find our final rest in Jesus.

Non-Biblical References and Notes

On occasion, as indicated below, I've consulted Wikipedia. I'm aware this can raise academic eyebrows, but for a non-scholar such as myself it's a valuable resource. For example, I'm inclined to think that someone who gives over a hundred references and a separate considerable list of original sources has given the topic in question careful study, and probably knows what she/he is talking about. I'm only sorry that I don't know their names in order to be able to acknowledge their work.

1. There are about two million Anabaptists/Mennonites in the USA and Canada, and three quarters of a million in Africa. Others are scattered throughout the world, in 86 countries. The 'shared convictions' which summarise Anabaptist beliefs are included as an Appendix at the end of this book.

2. Berry, Wendell. *Blessed are the Peacemakers.* (2005, Berkeley, Counterpoint)

3. To understand the full impact of the story of the Good Samaritan on those listening to Jesus, and to rediscover one of its most important messages, we

have to appreciate the intensity of the dislike and contempt 1st-century Jews and Samaritans had for each other, directly reflected today in the hostility between Israelis and Palestinians. (The sectarian divide in Ulster is another stark reminder of how centuries old antagonisms can become deeply ingrained in communities.) Jesus' questioner and the other listeners must have been shaken to be told that, in terms of God's Law, their neighbour was, of all people, a hated *Samaritan*; especially when the punchline was 'Go and do likewise.'

4. Stark, Rodney. *The Rise of Christianity*. (1997, New York, HarperOne.) Stark also gives fascinating insights into the realities of life in the Roman Empire which, incidentally, was remarkably cosmopolitan. Immaculate togas and sun-drenched villas, as depicted in many films about ancient Rome, were only for the very few. For most Roman citizens, and certainly for foreigners and slaves, life was hard, squalid, smelly, dangerous and short.

5. MacGregor, Kirk R. *Nonviolence in the Ancient Church and Christian Obedience*. (2008, Themelios, 33:1 (online journal))

6. Tertullian later softened this stance, to the effect that although baptised Christians could under no circumstances join the military, soldiers and public officials could become converts without resigning from their posts so long as they refused to enjoin

violence. How a serving soldier was expected to avoid involvement in violence was not made clear.

7. Murray, Stuart. *Post-Christendom*. (2018 (2nd Ed), London, SCM Press)

8. Constantine the Great. (2021, Wikipedia)

9. Theodosius I. (2021, Wikipedia)

10. The Conflict of Church and State in Europe 1035 to 1513. In: *The Times Atlas of World History* (1978, London, Times Books)

11. Augustine of Hippo. (2021, Wikipedia)

12. European Religious Wars. (2021, Wikipedia)

13. Zinsser, Hans. *Rats, Lice and History*. (1935, London, Routledge; 2017 repr London, Prelude) pp 274–280.

14. Dalrymple, William. From the Holy Mountain. (1997, London, HarperCollins)

15. *The Guardian* (newspaper) 14 December 2018

16. *The Observer* (newspaper) 6 January 2019

17. Hauerwas, Stanley and Willimon, William H. *Resident Aliens*. (1989, Nashville, Abingdon Press)

18. Christian Soldiers. Slate.com, 10 February 2015

19. The Jewish Diaspora, AD 70 to 1497. In: *The Times Atlas of World History* (1978, London, Times Books)

20. Wright, Tom. *Paul, a Biography*. (2018, London, SPCK)

21. Ponsonby, Simon. *God is For Us*. (2013, London, Monarch)

22. Stark, Rodney. *Bearing False Witness*. (2017, London, SPCK)

23. Anti-Jewish Pogroms in the Russian Empire. (2021, Wikipedia)

24. I'm aware that I'm invoking something like the Christus Victor theory of atonement here. Beyond observing that it seems to make sense in this context, it would be far above my theological pay grade to make any further soteriological comments.

25. Wright, NT. *Scripture and the Authority of God.* (2016, London, SPCK)

26. Berkhof, Hendrik. *Christ and the Powers.* (1977, Scottdale, and Waterloo, Herald Press) Originally published in Dutch in 1953.

27. Yoder, John Howard. *The Politics of Jesus.* (1972, Grand Rapids, Eerdmans)

28. Wink, Walter. *The Powers That Be.* (1998, New York, Doubleday)

29. Galtung, Walter. (2022, Wikipedia)

30. Hyung Jin Kim Sun. *Who Are Our Enemies and How Do We Love Them?* (2020, Harrisonburg, Herald Press)

31. Studdert Kennedy, GA. *The Unutterable Beauty*, 16th Edn. (1936, London, Hodder and Stoughton)

32. Wright, Tom. *Spiritual and Religious.* (2017, London, SPCK)

33. Stott, John. *Issues Facing Christians Today.* (1984, Basingstoke, Marshall)

34. Billings, Alan. *The Dove, the Figleaf and the Sword.* (2014, London, SPCK) Both the author, who has

taught the ethics of war to UK service chaplains, and the Foreword writer on the author's behalf, emphasise that 'the principal argument of this book is that ... Christianity ... was never a "pacifist" movement in any absolute sense.' Their 'principal argument' is simply, factually wrong. This obviously undermines much of what the book has to say, but it does unintentionally illustrate what Wink (28) meant by 'the infinitely malleable ideology of the just war'.

35. Remarque, Erich Maria. *All Quiet on the Western Front*. (1996, London, Vintage). A must-read book, brilliant for its depiction of the horrors of war. 'We set out as soldiers ... we reach the zone where the front line begins, and we have turned into human animals' (p 39). 'But we are dragged along forward again with everyone else, unwilling but crazed, wild and raging, we want to kill, because now the others are our deadly enemies, their grenades and rifles are aimed at us, and if we don't destroy them they will destroy us' (p 80). Remarque served in the German army in WW1. As well as vivid descriptions of front-line warfare based on his own experiences, he describes the distressing detachment from civilian life felt by soldiers returning home from the front.

36. Garcia, Cesar. *What is God's Kingdom, and What does Citizenship Look Like?* (2021, Harrisonburg, Herald Press). There are many challenges here. Garcia explores ideas around borders between kingdoms,

and about the nature of kingship as manifest in Jesus. I find especially attractive his suggestion that disciples of Jesus are ambassadors for God's kingdom. As a UK resident I also found helpful his take on the interface between religion and politics in the USA (he himself is Colombian).

37. Julian (Emperor) (2021, Wikipedia)

38. Herman, Nicholas (Brother Lawrence). *The Practice of the Presence of God*. (2015, Fairhope, Mockingbird Classics Publishing)

39. Woolman, John. *The Journal of John Woolman*. (1774. Modern edition from Pantianos Classics). He was an 18th-century North American colonist, and a Quaker. He campaigned tirelessly, and with success, to persuade his fellow Quakers in the colonies to give freedom to the slaves they owned. He also communicated, without violence, with several native Indian tribes at what he called a 'spiritual' level. In 1772 he visited England to continue his anti-slavery campaigning. While here he succumbed to smallpox, and died in York. His Journal has been continuously in print since it was first published in 1774.

40. Two people on my list of 'stars' were not Christians. Nelson Mandela, brought up as a Methodist, did not profess any religious faith. His lack of bitterness and refusal to recriminate after 27 years in gaol made possible a surprisingly peaceful end to apartheid in South Africa. Mahatma Gandhi was a profoundly

spiritual man, who probably understood and practised nonviolent protest better than anyone else. He is said to have remarked that the only people on earth who don't see Christ and his teachings as nonviolent are Christians. He also said, 'I love your Christ, but I do not love Christians because they are not like Christ.' Ouch! Jesus said, 'You will know them by their fruit' (Mat 7.16). Quite so.

41. Bonhoeffer, Dietrich. *The Cost of Discipleship*. (1959, London, SCM Press). In the context of nonviolence, Bonhoeffer's is a special and unusual case. He is remembered and revered throughout Europe and North America as having been an outstanding theologian and man of faith. He was a founding member of the Confessing Church in Germany in the 1930s. His book *The Cost of Discipleship*, first published in German in 1937, includes an exegesis of the Sermon on the Mount which is utterly uncompromising in its advocacy of nonviolence, in all circumstances without exception. Having returned to Germany from England and the USA, in 1943 Bonhoeffer became involved in a plot to assassinate Adolf Hitler, for which he was arrested, and executed in April 1945 at the age of 39. His death had nothing directly to do with his faith: that is to say, he did not die because he was a Christian. No written explanation of his actions has been found, but in conversation with a friend he said he would answer to God for

what he had done. Walter Wink commented (28), 'Two generations of Christians have held back from full commitment to nonviolence, citing Bonhoeffer as justification. I wonder if he would have joined the death plot had he known that it would have the effect of condoning redemptive violence in the eyes of so many Christians.'

42. Augsburger, David. *Dissident Discipleship*. (2006, Grand Rapids, Brazos Press)

43. This phrase is from the Collect for the second Sunday in Advent, in the 1552 Book of Common Prayer of the Church of England, where it refers to 'Holy Scripture'.

44. For anyone who doubts the extent and significance of the church/state entanglement in England, I recommend watching the episode 'The Bishops Gambit' in the BBC comedy series *Yes, Prime Minister*, in which Prime Minister Jim Hacker is involved in the appointment of a new C of E bishop. It's very funny, but also unsparing in its exposure of the ecclesiastical and spiritual absurdities involved in these interactions in real life. I understand it has become required viewing in some theological colleges.

45. While writing this book I've discovered, without a huge feeling of surprise, that I'm an Anabaptist, in that I can identify with all the 'Shared Convictions' (see Appendix). Indeed, I think the *only* part of that document which would make any evangelical

Christian pause, even for a moment, is what this book is about – the commitment to nonviolence.

46. A poignant war memorial stands on Platform 1 of Paddington Station in London. It's a life-size bronze statue of a young soldier, standing in full kit with feet apart, helmet askew, a greatcoat draped across his shoulders, and a long knitted scarf wound round his neck. He looks down to a letter, presumably from home, in his hands, and his expression is absorbed and wistful. I suggest that it's worth a visit, and a prayer, from anyone passing through the station who has a minute or two to spare.

47. It's probably not necessary to point out that Matthew's repeated use of 'Kingdom of *Heaven*', rather than 'Kingdom of God', arises from his preference as a Jew to avoid using the name of God directly. The meanings are exactly the same.

Appendix

(I have taken this verbatim from pages 75–76 of Hyung Jin Kim Sun's book *Who Are Our Enemies?* (30))

Shared Convictions

Mennonite World Conference, a global community of Christian churches that facilitates community between Anabaptist-related churches, offers these shared convictions that characterise Anabaptist faith.

By the grace of God, we seek to live and proclaim the good news of reconciliation in Jesus Christ. As part of the one body of Christ at all times and places, we hold the following to be central to our belief and practice:

1. God is known to us as Father, Son and Holy Spirit, the Creator who seeks to restore fallen humanity by calling a people to be faithful in fellowship, worship, service and witness.

2. Jesus is the Son of God. Through his life and teaching, his cross and resurrection, he showed us how to be faithful disciples, redeemed the world, and offers eternal life.

3. As a church, we are a community of those whom God's Spirit calls to turn us from sin, acknowledge Jesus

Christ as Lord, receive baptism upon confession of faith, and follow Christ in life.

4. As a faith community, we accept the Bible as our authority for faith and life, interpreting it together under Holy Spirit guidance, in the light of Jesus Christ to discern God's will for our obedience.

5. The Spirit of Jesus empowers us to trust God in all areas of life so we become peacemakers who renounce violence, love our enemies, seek justice and share our possessions with those in need.

6. We gather regularly to worship, to celebrate the Lord's Supper, and to hear the Word of God in a spirit of mutual accountability.

7. As a worldwide community of faith and life we transcend boundaries of nationality, race, class, gender and language. We seek to live in the world without conforming to the powers of evil, witnessing to God's grace by serving others, caring for creation, and inviting all people to know Jesus as Saviour and Lord.

In these convictions we draw inspiration from Anabaptist forbears of the 16th century, who modelled radical discipleship to Jesus Christ. We seek to walk in his name by the Power of the Holy Spirit, as we confidently wait Christ's return and the final fulfilment of God's Kingdom.

Adopted by Mennonite World Conference General Council, 15 March 2006

Author biography

 Michael Rogers has been a disciple of Jesus all his life. During his secondary and further education, his home was Lee Abbey in North Devon where his father, Geoffrey Rogers, was Warden. In his teens Michael made a personal commitment to nonviolence. He studied medicine, and was a paediatrician in the UK National Health Service for over 40 years.

In retirement, and blessed to date with good health, Michael has made time to pray, read and think about his faith. In particular he has studied the wider implications of nonviolence, and has become convinced that it should be near the centre of Christian discipleship. He believes he has been given a message to pass on, and has written this book to reach as many people as possible with what he has to say.

Michael's other activities in retirement have included his family, supporting his local rural church, making and listening to music, boat building and sailing.